ComputerTown

BRINGING COMPUTER LITERACY TO YOUR COMMUNITY

ComputerTown

BRINGING COMPUTER LITERACY TO YOUR COMMUNITY

Liza Loop
Julie Anton
Ramon Zamora

Reston Publishing Company, Inc.
A Prentice-Hall Company
Reston, Virginia

Library of Congress Cataloging in Publication Data

Loop, Liza.
  ComputerTown, bringing computer literacy to your
community.

  Includes index
  1. Computer literacy.   2. Computers — Study and
teaching.   3. Microcomputers — Study and teaching.
I. Anton, Julie.   II. Zamora, Ramon.   III. Title.
IV. Title: ComputerTown, bringing computer literacy
to your community.
QA76.9.C64L66   1983   001.64'.07'1   83-3332
ISBN 0-8359-0875-5 (pbk.)

ISBN 0-8359-0884-4

ComputerTown USA! is a computer literacy project of People's Computer Company, a nonprofit educational corporation. The material in this book is based on
work supported by the National Science Foundation under Grant No.
SED8015964. Any opinions, findings, conclusions, or recommendations expressed are those of the authors and do not necessarily reflect the views of the
National Science Foundation.

10 9 8 7 6 5 4 3 2 1

Printed in the United States of America.

Contents

To the Reader

This book is a collection of ideas and suggestions for people who want to learn more about computers – the small microcomputers that seem to be everywhere. You do not have to be familiar with computers to read this book. In fact, if you know nothing about microcomputers, this book can show you how to learn about them informally, in the comfort of your home, your local library, or community setting.

The ComputerTown project, since its inception in 1979, has helped organize a number of events providing hands-on, public access to microcomputers. This book collects and records the experiences of the project, and encourages you to learn about computers by creating computer events in your own community.

The book is organized like an extended scrapbook, capturing both the successes and failures of the project. We ask you to read through the material, and then sit down with a few friends and plan your own community experiments. We guarantee that if you implement just one "Computer Family Night" or similar event, you will learn a lot about microcomputers. Your experiences can be added to the scrapbook, expanding your local ability to bring technology to your community.

For people with computer experience, this book provides a rich resource of ideas on how to use your skills in a public access, community setting. The opportunities for someone wanting to help others learn about microcomputers are nearly boundless. Use this book to spark your teaching, organizing, and technical talents, right in your own home town. Consider becoming an official ComputerTown affiliate, and a member of the network of over 100 public access, community-based, computer literacy sites around the U.S. and the world.

No matter what your level of expertise may be regarding microcomputers, you will find this book informative, infectious, and inspiring. And, before you get to the last page, you may be the one who is "bringing computer literacy to your community."

— The Authors

Preface

We live in an era of accelerating change. Looking around us in the 1980's, we see the tools we mastered during childhood displayed as museum relics. Our books are outdated before we can buy them, much less read them. Word of events, both earth-shaking and trivial, reaches us within seconds from anywhere on the planet. How can we keep up with global change, living in our own local communities? How can we promote equal access to the tools of the future?

A ComputerTown is one answer to this set of questions, one way of providing people within a community with information and access to computer-based technologies.

The pages that follow present an album of verbal snapshots chronicling the development of many computer literacy activities. Most of the pictures come from the ComputerTown in Menlo Park, California. A few show our friends from around the world. The subjects of the pictures are activities, people, and resources.

We offer these experiences in this form so that the ComputerTown idea will grow and spread worldwide—a community of people making technology available to everyone. Within this book we extend our hand to you and encourage you to start your own ComputerTown projects. Why? So that you, your neighbors, and your children will walk confidently with us into the information age.

Few of the ideas in this book are original to the authors. For the most part, we have served as recorders, capturing on paper the images of others as they encountered technology. We thank everyone who has been part of the evolution of this project and regret that we are unable to list all of them by name. Instead, we invite you to watch for people and places mentioned throughout the text. Each citation and each inclusion in the resource list is an acknowledgement of our thanks and appreciation.

Each person who attended a ComputerTown event, workshop, or class has taught us something new. Each member of an audience who has asked us questions about the project and the technology has made a contribution to this document.

A declaration of special appreciation goes out to the hundreds of volunteers at all the ComputerTown sites who gave their time and know-how to do the real work of each project — carrying machines, mailing flyers, assisting in classes, cleaning keyboards, soliciting donations, and saying over and over again, "That's right; now press the key marked RETURN."

A specific recognition of contribution goes to the people who have worked as ComputerTown staff members, advisors, and helping hands on the Menlo Park project. They are:

STAFF

Julie Anton	Michael Madaj
Pat Cleland	Ann Merchberger
Jeanne Duprau	Niels Mortenson
Sue Eldredge	Martine Peyton-Boot
Barbara Harvie	Cheryl Rhodes
Fritzi Lareau	Bill Scarvie
Liza Loop	Clifford West

Ramon Zamora

ADVISORS

Ludwig Braun	Jane D. Gawronski

Bob Albrecht

HELPING HANDS AND CONTRIBUTORS

Holly Anderson	Dick Ricketts
Sharon Franklin	Pelton Steward
Matt Lehmann	David Tebbutt
Marlin Ouverson	David Thornburg
Dale Peterson	David Warren

MENLO PARK LIBRARY STAFF

Beata Bartholomay

Doreen Cohen

Robbie Fanning

Karen Frederickson

Dan Horne

Sue Rocca-Butler

Maryann Whiting

1

Welcome to
ComputerTown!

Let's begin by exploring a few of the basic concepts which form the foundation of the ComputerTown Project.

What is a ComputerTown?

A ComputerTown is any public access computer literacy project. It is a group of individuals, adults and children, helping each other become informed citizens of today's information society. A ComputerTown's goal is to offer an informal educational opportunity for everyone in the community to become "computer literate."

What Constitutes Computer Literacy at a ComputerTown Site?

The word "literate" has traditionally referred to a person who can read and write. Before the introduction of the many mechanical and electronic tools of the last eighty years, this definition was adequate.

Today a broader definition of literacy is necessary. This requirement surfaces each time we address the use of a mechanical or electronic tool. For example, a person who drives a car needs some reading and writing skills in order to get a driver's license. The process of driving, however, demands some other kind of basic "literacy."

3

Computer literacy at the ComputerTown, Menlo Park site focuses on providing hands-on computer experiences for the new to intermediate potential microcomputer user, assisting these people in becoming comfortable, aware, and informed about this technology.

ComputerTown classes, workshops, and hands-on situations are informal experiences facilitated by knowledgeable, friendly "driver-trainers." The staff deals primarily with familiarity rather than proficiency in their interactions during workshops and courses. When people are ready to "graduate" from the ComputerTown environment, the staff provides ideas, resources, and suggestions on where to turn for more information.

Who Benefits From a ComputerTown?

Anyone who would not otherwise have access to a computer or computer know-how benefits from a ComputerTown.

Children meeting microcomputers for the first time encounter a new tool for solving problems and expressing creativity. When a disadvantaged child discovers that he or she can program a computer, that child opens up a whole new spectrum of educational and vocational possibilities. Teenagers, many of whom are already computer literate, learn social and teaching skills. A ComputerTown provides a significant learning experience which broadens and supplements what a child learns in school. Knowledge is often passed on from child to parent.

Initial adult users with little experience often exhibit anxiety and discomfort when they first encounter the technology. An introductory set of workshops, courses, and hands-on experiences addresses their questions and concerns. The words "Computer Comfort" categorize this stage of the adult users' investigations. They look for some way to relate to the technology, some way to get comfortable with it, and ComputerTown shows them how.

Once a sense of comfort is established, users progress through a stage labeled "Computer Awareness." The focus at this and the previous level is not on proficiency but on familiarity with the technology. Knowledge at the experiential level, gained by hands-on activities, takes precedence over "hard" learning objectives, such as being able to program.

Once users are comfortable with the technology and aware of

the computer's capabilities, they are offered preliminary courses and workshops in "Computer Tool Use." Some of these activities might include learning to program the computer, experimenting with various computer languages, or adapting software packages for use within the home or small business.

At ComputerTown, Menlo Park, computer literacy activities stop at this point. This test site has concentrated on the new to intermediate user of the technology. Of course, ComputerTowns need not restrict their activities to these first three user stages. The impetus for ComputerTown, however, came from the discovery of the large number of people who wanted access to microcomputers and had no notion of where to begin their search. Most ComputerTown sites find it adequate, even a test of their resources, to try servicing this particular set of users exclusively.

The literacy approaches outlined for kids don't necessarily follow those for adults. As one person on the ComputerTown, USA! project noted, "You teach kids programming; you teach adults what to do with the machine, the applications." Most kids appear to be comfortable with the technology. Some kids possess an amazing awareness of microcomputers and technology in general. Kids prefer to learn, as quickly as possible, how to control and direct the machine using the available programming languages. They also like to play games on the computer.

At ComputerTown, Menlo Park, courses for kids involve the use of "games-with-a-purpose" and the teaching of the fundamentals of programming. Games-with-a-purpose are programs that combine implicit learning activities within a gaming context. Courses and workshops for kids are presented informally and emphasize exploration and experimentation.

ComputerTown offers adults a chance to take the first steps toward a career change, share a skill or hobby with others, or overcome shyness in the face of a new technology. For senior citizens, the handicapped, and others, computer literacy can open the way to fuller participation in today's world.

What Does a ComputerTown Do?

Each local ComputerTown determines its own activities. In its first two years, the ComputerTown in Menlo Park has conducted many classes, workshops, playdays, demonstrations,

ComputerTown offers adults a chance to take the first steps
toward a career change, share a skill or hobby with others, or overcome shyness in the face of a new technology.

question-and-answer sessions, special interest study groups, and lectures. Computers have traveled to the pizza parlor, the senior center, economically disadvantaged sectors of the community, and special education schools. ComputerTown, Menlo Park has also provided continuous public access to microcomputers at the public library, and its "Computer Validation" project certified more than 300 kids in the rudiments of microcomputer operation over a twelve month period.

Still more projects are in the idea stage at Menlo Park: Rent-a-Computer (to use at home); Rent-a-Computerkid (to teach you how); tours of computing facilities; neighborhood computer clubs; show-and-tell meetings; video game contests; programmable vehicle rodeos; and a mentor program to find computer professionals who will work with advanced learners.

There are no specific requirements for ComputerTown activities. They grow and develop according to community need and interest.

Where Is a Typical ComputerTown Located?

A ComputerTown can be most anywhere. It is an informal learning environment, with all the variation that entails. All it takes is for someone to set up a computer where people can learn through hands-on experience, and suddenly you have a ComputerTown site.

In one community, ComputerTown may be only a common interest shared by independent people who decide to make computers available for public use—without a special place of residence. Another ComputerTown could be a formal organization which has officers, a well-defined program of activities, a place of business, and equipment. Some ComputerTowns are located at libraries, recreation centers, senior centers, or other public facilities. Others may promote computer literacy with the support of private groups, computer stores, computer hobbyist clubs, or schools and colleges.

Are There Any ComputerTowns Yet?

Quite a few exist already, and the list continues to grow. ComputerTown, Menlo Park, located in the public library, has been

promoting computer literacy since 1979. There is a Computer-
Town in Florida, one in Oklahoma, one in Illinois, several in the
United Kingdom, and many others around the United States
which share the spirit, if not the name, of ComputerTown.

A complete list of present ComputerTowns can be found in
Appendix D. For more up-to-date information, write to ComputerTown International, P.O. Box E, Menlo Park, California
94025.

What Is ComputerTown, USA!?

In September, 1981, ComputerTown, USA! became a nationwide
project of People's Computer Company, funded by the National
Science Foundation. Its job has been to conduct an experimental
computer literacy project in the Menlo Park Public Library and to
encourage the development of new ComputerTowns by providing
support in three forms:

1. Publication of the periodical called *The ComputerTown,
   USA! News Bulletin.*
2. Development of an implementation package containing
   information on how to start and manage a successful
   ComputerTown.
3. Creation of an informal network among the Computer-
   Town affiliates.

In response to public interest, the staff of ComputerTown,
USA! went on to form an organization called ComputerTown International.

What Is ComputerTown International?

While ComputerTown, USA! is a short-term, experimental project of limited scope, ComputerTown International plans to extend
the range of products and services offered to potential Computer-
Town organizers on a long-term basis. Regional Community
Coordinators will locate human and computer-based resources to

ComputerTowns can be only a common interest shared by independent people or they can be formal organizations that have officers, a
well-defined program of activities, a place of business, and equipment. Some ComputerTowns are located at libraries, recreation
centers, senior centers, or other public facilities.

facilitate the formation of ComputerTowns. In addition to a bi-monthly bulletin, ComputerTown International is creating a series of ComputerTown books for beginners.

ComputerTown International is a membership organization that accepts contributions. Funds are applied to the support of computer literacy activities throughout the world.

Why Do We Need ComputerTowns?

David Tebbutt,* who helped develop the British ComputerTown network (ComputerTown, UK!), puts it this way:

> We need a wide acceptance and familiarity with computers among the population at large. ComputerTown provides a completely nonthreatening and fun way of bringing this about. In the future, our children will be thinking in ways that we can't even envision at the moment. The computer is providing them with an intellectual tool that they can drive and control to achieve mental feats which we would probably consider absurd — if we knew what they were likely to be! Our approach to ComputerTown is intended to create an environment in which this can happen.

The History of ComputerTown

The first ComputerTown began in 1979 as the local community experiment of Bob Albrecht and Ramon Zamora, who were writing books on elementary computer programming. In order to observe ordinary people exploring computers for the first time, Bob and Ramon brought microcomputers to pizza parlors, bookstores, parks, and their local public library. What they saw not only improved their manuscripts, but provided hours of pleasure to the kids and adults who played computer games and learned

*Reprinted with permission from "Why Do We Need ComputerTowns?" which appears in the *ComputerTown, UK! Guidelines*, February 1980, by David Tebbutt. Human Skills, 7 Collins Drive, Eastcote, Middlesex, UK, HA4 9EL.

BASIC language commands. Soon the computers and their collection of preprogrammed game tapes found a permanent home in the Menlo Park Public Library. The dream of making Menlo Park, California the first completely "computer literate" community began to take shape. They called the project "Computer-Town, USA!"

ComputerTown, USA! was by no means the first public access computer literacy project. However, its friendly, informal approach attracted national press coverage and the attention of the National Science Foundation's (NSF) Development in Science Education Project. Late in 1979, the project staff sent an informal proposal to the National Science Foundation requesting funding for activities. NSF requested a more formal proposal, and by 1980, ComputerTown, USA! was officially sponsored by the National Science Foundation. Zamora was awarded a grant to develop ComputerTown into a demonstration computer literacy project, to disseminate the Menlo Park model to libraries and other institutions as widely as possible, and to promote the formation of other ComputerTown sites across the United States.

With the inception of ComputerTown, UK! in Great Britain, the project surpassed its original goals, becoming an international computer literacy network. The British ComputerTown affiliate network was launched in the November, 1980 issue of *Personal Computer World* magazine. Fifteen ComputerTown projects mushroomed throughout the United Kingdom in the first six months, and two existing computer clubs became affiliated with ComputerTown, UK!.

Taking their lead from suggestions published in the ComputerTown *News Bulletin*, still other projects began to appear. The Palo Alto (California) Junior Museum presented a month-long computer exhibit, and began to offer classes on computer literacy in conjunction with the city's community services program.

"Computers for Senior Citizens," implemented by volunteer Matt Lehmann in conjunction with Menlo Park's Little House Senior Center, went on to join forces with Joan Targ's Palo Alto-based "Computer Tutor" program. As a result of this merger, young people began to work with the seniors on a set of time-sharing terminals supplied with the aid of a local foundation. Participating seniors could go on to become full-fledged "Computer Tutors" themselves.

The Herbert Hoover Boys' Club, also in Menlo Park, received a Commodore computer, donated by Bob Albrecht, which proved so popular with club members that the club obtained several more and offered daily computer access as a regular service. One young man at the Boys' Club observed, "If they had computers when I was in school, I'd probably still be there!"

Holly Anderson of Barrington, Illinois, is a parent who began to promote computer litercy in her local school system, and went on to found ComputerTown, Barrington. The project's kick-off event was a conference for over five hundred teachers and educators.

Several other public access computer literacy projects share the spirit of ComputerTown. One such project is based at The Capital Children's Museum in Washington, D.C. With the donation of thirty computers by Atari, Inc. in 1981, the museum began to use computers in its communication exhibits. It also established computer literacy classes in programming and computer play. The museum staff also initiated comprehensive computer literacy classes for members of Congress. Museum visitors may use the KidNet computerized message system, made possible by a grant from Digital Equipment Corporation. "Superboots," the museum's software development project, is producing a series of educational book/software packages which let visitors take the spirit home.

By the fall of 1982, the network of ComputerTowns and ComputerTown affiliates numbered over one hundred sites throughout the world. In addition to those just described, this network includes the Center for Mathematics Literacy at San Francisco State University, the San Bernadino, California Public Library, the Chicago Public Library, the Austin Public Library, the Norman, Oklahoma Public Library (ComputerTown, OK!), and others.

When ComputerTown's founders took their first machines to the pizza parlor, they learned that when people come together with computers in a comfortable, exploratory setting, new discoveries are bound to be made — not only about the fundamentals of the technology, but about all kinds of possible applications. It is not all that unusual these days to walk into a ComputerTown site and find a teen-aged programmer deep in thought and exploration. While he may only be writing the simplest of programs, he is part of a wave of people learning to use and shape the technologies of the future. ComputerTowns have made it possible for thousands of individuals to discover the power and current limitations of today's microcomputer.

2

Planning Your ComputerTown

The first ComputerTowns simply evolved. The original volunteers did not invest a lot of effort in planning or setting specific goals, since their purpose was primarily experimental. Now that the exploratory cycle is over, however, ComputerTown International recommends a certain amount of planning before activities begin.

If you are familiar with computers and have decided to share your interest and knowledge, you probably have your own ideas on how to begin a ComputerTown project. But what if you've never touched a computer? You can still take steps toward establishing a computer literacy project. Begin by gathering information. Visit local computer clubs. Explore your town for likely places to house a public access computer project. Find a partner to share ideas, tasks, knowledge, and resources. Don't let a lack of technical know-how slow you down. You will become more expert as the project develops.

If you are comfortable with computers and have some available equipment, you may want to follow the lead of the first ComputerTowns by jumping right into an experimental operation. If you prefer a solid structure, lack experience, or need equipment and funds, devote a certain amount of time to planning. Be forewarned, though, that due to their informal nature, ComputerTowns often take on a life of their own. Plan what you would like to see happen and adjust the plans as things develop.

Six key elements emerged during ComputerTown experiments in the Menlo Park Library and other local sites. If you intend to take a structured approach to the ComputerTown model, consider the following ComputerTown ingredients in your plans:

- A ComputerTown mayor
- Two mayoral assistants
- Access to at least one microcomputer
- A friendly public access host institution
- Rules and regulations
- Local newspaper contact

Let's take a look at them individually.

The ComputerTown Mayor

Every ComputerTown needs a mayor. This is the person in charge of it all, the person with "vision." It would be helpful if the ComputerTown mayor were computer literate from the outset, but if not, he or she will quickly learn. The only important prerequisite for a ComputerTown mayor is commitment.

The ComputerTown mayor is in charge of administration and organization. With a finger on the pulse of all ComputerTown happenings, the mayor is also an ace communicator. "There will be a ComputerTown Playday at Johnson School Multipurpose Room on Saturday, February 18th, from 10 a.m. to 3 p.m.," the mayor might announce at town meeting. "Call me for further details. Do we have any volunteers?" When the big day arrives, the mayor makes that extra run to the hardware store to pick up the electrical plug converter and later passes the hat for donations.

If the ComputerTown has no permanent headquarters, the mayor's own home could be a temporary base of operation. The mayor could install a special telephone for interested callers, or offer his or her own existing number for the calls. The mayor might rent a post office box for the ComputerTown mail, or offer the garage for storage. When the group finds its permanent site, the mayor takes charge of organizing operations.

Energetic, committed, willing to roll up their sleeves when there's work to be done, ComputerTown mayors must also know how to delegate responsibility among ComputerTown citizens. A good working rapport between the mayor and other volunteers is very important, especially as ComputerTown begins to grow.

Two Mayoral Assistants

The ComputerTown mayor should ideally be supported by at least two "mayoral assistants." One or both should be knowledgeable about microcomputers and willing to teach, especially if the mayor is still learning about the technology. At least one assistant should have access to a computer and be willing to take it to ComputerTown activities.

The mayoral assistants (and anyone else who instructs or facilitates at ComputerTown events) must be able to operate a computer in a public situation. A situation where fifteen kids are all jostling to play a game on one computer requires someone with the skills of a diplomatic referee. Working with groups of people new to the technology often requires great tact and patience. The assistants must be flexible enough to act as diplomats, arbitrators, and teachers in the public access setting.

The assistants should be familiar enough with the equipment to know which pieces to bring to a ComputerTown event, recognize problems with the hardware or software, and know what to do if problems occur. In the event of a complete breakdown, for example, the plucky assistant may give a spontaneous lesson in beginning programming without the use of a computer!

One assistant should be willing to serve as backup in any capacity, especially if he or she is not computer literate. This may mean greeting people at the door to announce that tonight's ComputerTown meeting has been cancelled because the computer is down with an undiagnosed disease, making and posting signs, rallying volunteers at the mayor's request, or "shushing" noisy Adventure players in the library reading room.

Like those of the mayor and other volunteers, the assistants' tasks may run from the glorious to the mundane. They must have energy, commitment, and a good rapport with their fellow volunteers.

Access to One Computer

Some computer literacy events can actually take place without a computer, but most people will want to see, touch, and operate the real thing for themselves. If you start the project without a computer, field trips to banks, computer stores, automated offices, and school data processing departments can keep your new ComputerTown busy while you locate a microcomputer or time-share terminal to use on an occasional basis. There is probably an individual or two in your town who would be willing to bring a personal computer for a show-and-tell meeting. You can build from there. Meanwhile, the important thing is not to wait until your group owns several computers. Start now. The rest will come in time.

A Friendly Public Access Host: The "Town Hall"

A ComputerTown "town hall" has two major functions: as a contact point for information, and a gathering place for activities.

A post office box or the address and phone number of one of the members will serve admirably for your brand new Computer-Town's information contact point. If you use a private address, try to find someone willing to provide mail and phone headquarters for six months to a year. Be aware that calls and letters will continue to arrive there even after your ComputerTown has established its own permanent address.

A private residence will serve as an adequate site of activities if nothing else is available, but a public facility would be much better. As you search for a suitable public access host site, examine the sorts of events and activities you want to present. Evaluate traffic, security, supervision, time schedules, and any other appropriate considerations. Once you have carefully assessed your needs, consider the public access sites available in your community. Narrow the choices down to those which seem best suited to ComputerTown's needs, and ask for permission to conduct events there.

Chances are, you will find more than one suitable and willing ComputerTown host. If so, all the better! Some sites are more suited to certain groups and activities, so don't hesitate to work with more than one ComputerTown host. Adult groups, for instance, may function best in an auditorium or seminar room. Children need a friendly place to let off a little steam. Check your local laws and regulations on room capacity and responsible adult-to-child ratio. These laws vary from county to county. For small children, the elderly, or the handicapped, stairs might be a problem. Computers, of course, require many electrical outlets and relatively consistent power — a prime consideration in any prospective ComputerTown site.

Be sure to give the hosts full credit and publicity for their participation in any event. Distinguish between "joint events" and events sponsored by ComputerTown at the host's facilities. Joint events should have dual billing on posters, announcements, and other publicity. Volunteers and staff from both ComputerTown and the host will deserve acknowledgement and thanks for their efforts. Grateful recognition will ensure that they look forward to working with you agian.

Rules and Regulations

Even if your ComputerTown has a very informal structure, a few established rules and procedures will probably be necessary. The simplest way to inform visitors of ComputerTown rules is to post them near the computers. The following list was posted at the Menlo Park test site:

ComputerTown, Menlo Park
Computer Rules

1. You must have a current library card from any library and a validation stamp on the back, signed and dated by a ComputerTown staff member.
2. Fill out the sign-up sheet completely. Enter your full name and the starting and finishing times in the columns under the name and number of the computer you will be using.
3. There is a half-hour limit on your computer time if other people are waiting.
4. Two people (not three) may sign up together — one for the first half hour and the other for the last half hour, and actually have a full hour together.
5. You get one half-hour session per day unless there is no one waiting to use the computer.

6. Please take care of the computers and library facilities — no food, gum, drinks, or littering are allowed in the library or near the computers. ESPECIALLY DRINKS!

7. Always rewind and return tapes to the tape box.

8. Pay attention to aides and librarians — penalties can include loss of computer time.

In addition to the posted rules, the ComputerTown project kept a pad of paper available for visitors to jot down suggestions for further information, resources, events, and services they would like to see at the ComputerTown site.

Some special problems can occur when kids use computers at a ComputerTown. They often lose track of time spent at the computers, and may have to be reminded that their time is up and someone else would like a turn. Since kids tend to crowd around the computers, there may be a noise and congestion problem. Kids sometimes need assistance with loading tapes; tapes and their covers may get mixed up.

These problems can be eased by separating the children's computers from the adults', and by providing an adult Computer-Town representative in the kids' section to answer questions, solve disputes, and generally supervise activities. Although an age-limit policy may not be necessary at your site, the Menlo Park library reserved two computers for children aged two through nine, when accompanied by a parent. Unsupervised use of computers by children under nine was restricted to those who could pass the validation tests.

Evolve your own set of rules and procedures based on your experiences in working with the public. In time, you will discover the appropriate regulations for your own situation and group of computer users.

Local Newspaper Contact

If people know that they are invited to learn about computers at your ComputerTown, they will come. Your best message carrier is the local events calendar of your home town newspaper. Plan

Some special problems can occur when kids use computers at a ComputerTown. They often lose track of time and may have to be reminded to give someone else a turn. Since kids tend to crowd around the computer, there may be a noise and congestion problem. These problems can be eased by separating the children's computers from the adults' and by providing a staff member to supervise.

your event two to three weeks in advance and call the newspaper with the pertinent information: what, where, when, who, for whom. Computer literacy is hot news for the 1980s, so ask for top billing and you are likely to get it. Additional publicity through a few well-placed posters in bookstores, computer stores, community centers, schools, and various bulletin boards and kiosks around town will more than likely cause your meeting room to overflow.

Once you have finished the planning stage, there's nothing to it but to do it! Each ComputerTown grows from the resources available to its founders and responds to its own community's needs. The following sections describe events, activities, and projects successfully undertaken by ComputerTowns so far. As you read, choose a few that seem within your grasp, considering the resources presently at hand. Starting with these, add new activities as your ComputerTown population grows.

No matter how eager you may be to get rolling, remember to be sensible about the number of staff and amount of effort your plan will require. There is no need to start big. A few carefully scattered seeds will grow naturally. If you schedule one afternoon event each quarter, for instance, your ComputerTown has begun. Encourage those who attend your first event to help organize future activities. Before you know it, you will have a flourishing ComputerTown.

3

The Gentle Art of
Offering Events

A ComputerTown event lasting one day or less is an ideal way to introduce the fundamentals of computer literacy to beginners. A one-day event has several functions:

- It provides many people with their first introduction to computing and computer literacy.
- It facilitates this introduction in a nonthreatening environment, and requires no further commitment on anyone's part.
- It puts ComputerTown volunteers in contact with others who would like to learn, teach, or organize future activities.

David Tebbutt, of ComputerTown, UK, offers these insights into the gentle art of conducting an introductory event:*

The important thing is to have fun and not to force the technology down people's throats. Let them become familiar with the machines by playing with them and talking to other people at ComputerTown. If anyone asks for more information, by all means talk things through with him, but in my view the whole thing should be at the visitor's own pace. I regularly give people a short introduction to the principles of

*Reprinted with permission from "Why Do We Need ComputerTowns?" which appears in the *ComputerTown, UK! Guidelines*, February 1980, by David Tebbutt. Human Skills, 7 Collins Drive, Eastcote, Middlesex, UK, HA4 9EL.

programming and lend them a self-instruction course so that they can learn in their own good time. Other members of my group introduce visitors to the principles of operating the machines, and after a suitable introduction will probably recommend appropriate reading for further information.

You see, ComputerTown is a pretty free and easy affair with the visitor learning at his or her own pace. We find that children and adults are quite different in their attitudes, with children being happy to learn by experimentation and discovery whereas adults find this process a little unnerving at first. Adults also feel a little embarrassed sometimes at participating in ComputerTown activities when there are so many kids around who are clearly quite knowledgeable about computing. I can only suggest that if this is a problem in your community, then you should perhaps hold some adult-only sessions.

Introductory Events

The following list of events held jointly by ComputerTown, Menlo Park and other organizations illustrates a range of possible ways to get people and computers together. Feel free to recreate them in your own community, and don't be reluctant to try new ideas of your own.

- *Herbert Hoover Boys' Club, East Menlo Park, California.* ComputerTown volunteers carried machines into this lower-income community center and provided about forty youths with hands-on access to microcomputers.
- *Sequoia School District, Menlo Park, California.* ComputerTown assisted with a Math/Science Day that doubled as an integration event for 250 kids in grades five and six. ComputerTown was the major source of equipment and software for the event.
- *Armstrong School, Ladera, California.* ComputerTown carried microcomputers into a classroom of eight children at this school for the learning disabled.

- *Ormondale School, Portola Valley, California.* ComputerTown helped augment a Media Center Computer Day for kids and parents, providing software and machines for over sixty visitors.
- *Learning Faire, Peninsula School, Menlo Park, California.* For two consecutive years, ComputerTown personnel helped set up and design a large hands-on microcomputer area as part of the school's annual Learning Faire. Both years, approximately five hundred fairgoers used the microcomputers.
- *Street Fair, Menlo Park, California.* The city's annual Street Fair included a ComputerTown table, offering about one hundred people a chance to use one of the several different kinds of microcomputers provided by the project. Portions of ComputerTown's activities that day were filmed for the television program, "Don't Bother Me, I'm Learning."

In a six-month period, ComputerTown contacted nearly a thousand people at these events, as well as additional hundreds at workshops, classes, and library open access events. Building on the success of these and other events, ComputerTown at Menlo Park has gone on to provide thousands of people with hands-on computer experiences. You, too, can reach out to a large number of people in your area. Start with a few of these suggested events or create your own and let the momentum that develops tell you what to do next.

Special Workshops

Special workshops on specific themes will enhance the scope and quality of your computer literacy activities. ComputerTown, Menlo Park supplemented its hands-on introductory events with the following workshops.

- *Creativity Workshops.* ComputerTown, Menlo Park offered "Kid's Creativity Workshops" at the library. These workshops let kids explore the worlds of fantasy and imagination with or without the use of a microcomputer. They became experiments in alternative ways to integrate kids and computers into the library setting.

A typical workshop of this kind would begin with one of the many versions of "Adventure." Once the kids had a general idea of how the game was played, facilitators would ask them to start the game again, without outside help, so that they could learn to use the computers independently. As the play continued, facilitators would suggest that the players create paper-and-pencil maps of locations, in order to encourage an awareness of the network structure embedded in the game.

These computer games were augmented by verbal fantasy role-playing games where the children were encouraged to explore an alternate cave-like structure. In the verbal games, they had to decipher a number of verbal clues and use their answers to create a map of the network they were exploring.

These fantasy games and active fantasy/imagination exercises provided a natural bridge between standard library programs, such as story hours, and the Computer-Town activities.

- *Family Days.* While many activities at the Menlo Park test site were geared toward adults or children, special "Family Day" events were also presented, in which people of all ages were encouraged to explore the technology together. "Family Day" events provided a unique setting in which the more adept children had a rare opportunity to teach the grownups something about computer technology.

- *Computer Workshops for Women and Girls.* Computer-Town staff observed that only about fifteen percent of those who came to the library site to use computers were female. In order to encourage more women and girls to become aware of the availability and potential of the technology and get involved with the ComputerTown project, a special workshop entitled "Computers for Women and Girls" was held at the Menlo Park Library. With the help of a local women's resource group that pitched in with publicity and volunteers, the workshop was a success.

Some fifty visitors, most of whom had no previous experience with microcomputers, were relaxed and eager to learn in the nonthreatening environment.

Working with Volunteers

Volunteers are the backbone of a successful ComputerTown and successful ComputerTown events. In every community, there are plenty of people who are willing to give time to an exciting project that provides community access to computers. Willing volunteers require a structure for their efforts, however. They also require positive results and feedback from their work. After all, success is their only payment!

Try to assign each volunter a job appropriate to his or her abilities. People with no computer experience can help organize, post notices, or be hosts at the events. They will pick up computer skills just by being around, but you can offer an orientation class to volunteers to speed up the process.

If you expect commitment from volunteers, clearly define your needs. Make a list of tasks which could be done by volunteers. Include the specific skills required and the name of the staff person in need of help. If at all possible, appoint one person to be volunteer coordinator. This person can make introductions, rally people for one-time events, schedule people for ongoing functions, and make sure that each volunteer is recognized and thanked for his or her contribution.

Be specific when asking for help: "I need people to act as hosts for newcomers at Family Night next Tuesday, between 6:30 and 8:45 p.m. They will greet people at the door, show them where to find the computers, books, software, and sign-up sheet. They will also tell people about upcoming activities and introduce them to the guest computer consultant. You need not be computer literate to handle this job. Please sign up with the volunteer coordinator as soon as possible, so that we can finalize the schedule by the first of the month."

People with computer experience bring one useful ingredient to your project: know-how. They can serve as consultants, tutors, mentors, maintenance crew, and sources of contact with commercial

Volunteers are the backbone of a successful ComputerTown and successful ComputerTown events. Try to assign each volunteer a job appropriate to his or her abilities. People with no computer experience can help organize, post notices, and host events. Those with computer experience can serve as consultants, tutors, mentors, maintenance crew, or as sources of contact with commercial organizations.

organizations. Let them know how valuable they are to ComputerTown.

Here are a few pitfalls to avoid when working with computer literate volunteers:

- Remember that microcomputers are new and take a little getting used to if someone has only worked on large, or older, computing systems. If you have microcomputers at your ComputerTown, suggest that "mainframe" people spend a little time with the manuals for each machine before they begin to teach. This will ensure that the information they offer beginners is accurate for microcomputers.

- Knowing how to do something is very different from knowing how to teach it to someone else. Try to identify the sensitive and natural teachers among your volunteers and use them effectively. Don't be overly impressed by someone who knows a lot but can't get it across. This problem sometimes occurs when a person has a moderate grasp of computing techniques, but has trouble handling group teaching situations. One solution could be to team these individuals with more experienced teachers.

- Beware of the person who volunteers to attend classes about computers, but frowns when you ask for help with clerical or non-computing tasks. Some "volunteers" are looking for free job training.

- One final note of caution: burn-out is a common malady for both volunteers and staff. Try not take on projects which outpace the available people power. Don't build an ongoing project around a single volunteer without considerable forethought and discussion. Let major projects unfold slowly and build on the enthusiasm in your community.

Typical ComputerTown Events

ComputerTown events don't just happen. Arranging a meeting space, collecting volunteers, deciding what sort of activities to offer, rounding up equipment and making sure that it gets there and back in working order, dealing with electrical outlets, taking care of publicity, and seeing that it all runs smoothly when the big day arrives—this myriad of details requires careful planning, coordination, strong nerves, and even a certain amount of muscle.

For an inside look at what goes into the process of planning and conducting a ComputerTown event, this section profiles volunteers' experiences in conducting four different presentations: a "Business Night" event, a presentation at a community "Learning Faire," a word processing study group, and a conference on computer literacy.

Profile 1: Business Night—Getting It All Together

Although it received minimal advertising, the Business Night workshop was one of the best attended events put on by ComputerTown, USA!. A few modest announcements went into local papers and $20.00 worth of flyers were distributed about town. The large attendance was a surprise, both to ComputerTown and library staff members. No one could remember a time when a brief, drop-in activity had drawn so many people to the Menlo Park Public Library. One contributing factor was undoubtedly its timely subject matter. Another factor makes this event especially worthy of a closer look: Business Night was well orchestrated.

The following memorandum, passed among the staff who planned the workshop, shows the kind of attention to detail which goes into the planning of a successful ComputerTown workshop. If you are planning a ComputerTown event, use the points in the memo as a model for an "Event Checklist" of your own. Expand the checklist as your ComputerTown grows. It will keep volunteers sane in the face of threatening chaos, and serve as a guide to future generations of ComputerTown volunteers. Copies of written memoranda such as this, filed for the benefit of future ComputerTown members, will also make their workload a lot easier.

Sample ComputerTown Event Memorandum

To: ComputerTown Volunteers
From: Ralph

Re: Business Night at the library

I've contacted several organizations with very good results so far ... IBM's General Systems Division will be delighted to attend. They'll bring their desktop computer with a printer. They will have a CAI course on how to operate the 5120, and a payroll package.

A representative of the Radio Shack Computer Center in San Mateo will also attend with a TRS-80 Model II. He's not sure what software he will bring. Someone from Heathkit's Redwood City store will come with the H89 "all in one" machine with a printer. That will make a great comparison to the IBM 5120!

The Digital Deli of Mountain View will bring the Intertec Superbrain with a Spinwriter (their own package 8995 deal).

Hewlett-Packard said they'd like to send someone, but will have to get back to us. I expect they will show up with one of their desktop machines. I intend to ask them to bring a plotter if possible.

Harry's Apple with Visicalc gives us six and probably seven systems from as many makers. A very educational variety! It also means a few practical problems ... A safe estimate is fifteen grounded plugs needing outlets from which they will draw as much as fifty amps. To avoid any chance of an embarrassing blown fuse, we ought to provide four 15-amp circuits. How do we get in touch with the Civic Center's electrician?

We'll have seven exhibitors plus two or three of us. We should have name tags which will help the visitors know who can answer a question and who is just another looker.

Getting all the people and machines in the room needs thought. What if we draw the wagons in a circle with the systems facing out, the attendees circling around the edges, and the exhibitors in the center?

Give me a call if you need help with the advertising. Should we invite the *Recorder* to send a reporter? Just a reminder: we need to have the media invitations and press releases out by the 17th. Who will contact the business groups in the area? And what about the electrical layout of the library? Where will we get sufficient extension cords and sockets? We'll need to arrange for tables and other paraphernalia like nametags. We will also need to deal with flyers and follow-up calls and letters to confirm and inform exhibitors. Please drop me a memo listing any other points that will need to be covered.

When inviting outside people to be presenters at a Computer-Town event, a personal phone call and an informal, follow-up letter are appropriate. The letter reproduced below went to guest presenters who had committed to attend the Business Night event. Feel free to use it as a model for your own invitations.

Sample Letter to Guest Presenters

Memo to: Participants, Business Night at the Menlo Park Library, Sponsored by ComputerTown _____
Day, Month, Year

Dear _____ ,

Thanks for agreeing to participate in Business Night. You'll find enclosed a map and a copy of the flyer we've sent out to the business and professional people of Menlo Park. This memo covers the points you should keep in mind while preparing your presentation.

The aim of Business Night, as with all ComputerTown projects, is education — in this case, the education of the Menlo Park business community in the practical benefits that computers could bring to their work. Education is the essence of Computer-Town, but its spirit has always been the idea that computers are fun. This won't be a heavy conference, but a casual evening among friends.

The event will take place in a conference room that is only about 16 by 22 feet in size. Since this is our first such venture we didn't aim any higher; if we are overcrowded we'll be pleased, and will immediately begin planning a better show in bigger surroundings.

The physical limits do bring up two considerations. First, plan to bring only one compact system, and to have only one person in attendance (although you will want to have a helper when setting up and tearing down). The room will be ready at 6:00 p.m.; try to arrive about that time. We all have to be out the door by 8:59 sharp, so plan to begin tearing down at 8:45 p.m.

Electrical power may be in short supply. The room is served by a single, 20-amp circuit. We hope this will be enough but we want to be prepared in case it is not. During set-up we will assign systems randomly to "A" and "B" groups. If the power is inadequate we'll alternate running the printers of the A and B groups each half-hour. If there still aren't enough watts then we will be forced to run the systems themselves in half-hour turns, beginning at 6:45.

We have some multi-socket extension cords, but more would be useful. Do bring handouts or brochures. Handing out computer-printed material is a great idea, but keep the power problem in mind and print up a batch beforehand. There may be a representative from the local press, so you might polish up your one-line answers to the question, "What's a computer, really?"

With everyone's cooperation Business Night can be a great success and lead to more of the same. See you then.

Regards,

Elaine Williams
Event Coordinator

Business Night brought over 200 people to the Menlo Park Library. A similar event in your area should be equally well attended.

Profile 2: Computers at the Learning Faire

Another successful ComputerTown, Menlo Park, event took place at the Peninsula School's annual Learning Faire. In the following article, author and ComputerTown volunteer David Thornburg describes the event:*

Each year the Peninsula School in Menlo Park, California conducts a "Learning Faire" for children, parents, teachers and neighbors. This year the Faire was held on May 4 and was attended by more than a thousand people who came to enjoy the food and music, learn about solar energy, make kites and candles, and to take part in myriad other activities including playing with computers. While the computer

*From "Computers at The Learning Faire" by David Thornburg. *COMPUTE!*, Vol. 1, Issue 5, July/August 1980, pp. 8-9. Reprinted with permission from *COMPUTE!* magazine, P.O. Box 5406, Greensboro, NC 27403. Copyright 1980 by Small Systems Services, Inc.

activity was a small part of the overall event, it was an enjoy-able, if exhausting, task for those of us who put it together.

The computer activity was planned by the Peninsula School Computer Project, ComputerTown, USA! and Inno-vision. We intended to present a computer activity which was smoothly integrated in spirit with other activities at the Faire including leather work, face painting, and events naturally suited to a fair conducted in a semi-rural environment on a beautiful spring day. The goal of the computer activity was to provide an opportunity for people of all ages to learn about computers and play games without feeling intimidated by these machines. This activity was to be used by everyone from computer experts to people who had never before seen a computer of any kind.

There were three major tasks which faced us as planners of this event. First, we needed to have enough hardware available to give every interested person a chance to use the machines. Second, we needed software which was appealing to boys and girls, young and old alike. Third, we needed enough volunteers to help people with the computers and to keep everything in working order.

Since we could only provide eight computers ourselves, we sought additional support from the outside. Through the generosity of Commodore, Atari, and Radio Shack, we were able to have more than twenty-five computers running at one time. This allowed us to run one program per machine—a blessing when one considers the time spent just loading tapes.

The software included stimulating games of many types, with the exception that no arcade-type games were used. Our reluctance to use arcade games was based on sev-eral factors. First, the majority of arcade games with which we were familiar were sufficiently "addictive" to certain chil-dren (primarily boys) that we could envision problems in providing easy access to the computers. More importantly, these games generally require very little cognitive activity on the part of the player, and were thus not considered appro-priate for incorporation in a "learning" fair. The most con-vincing argument against the use of these games, however, is that we were able to find a tremendous number of games which were fun, mentally stimulating, and appealing to people with little or no previous exposure to computers. This software included adventure games like TAIPAN and QUEST, logic games like BUTTON BUTTON, BRAIN BUSTER, QWERT, and MOTIE, simulations like LEMONADE, word games like WORDSEARCH, and creative environments like DRAW, just to mention a few of the programs which were in use that day.

We received tremendous assistance from the many volunteers who kept everything running smoothly. Volunteers included interested parents and several local computer professionals who enjoy working with children. This support allowed us to set aside a few machines for visitors who wanted to learn a little about computer programming. We also set aside two computers for the exclusive use of preschoolers.

In addition to the mixture of Commodore, Atari, Apple, and Radio Shack computers, we had several "outdoor" computer activities as well. Visitors to the computer area were treated to the beautiful sounds from two Alpha Syntauri computer music systems which were set up on Apples out under the arching oak trees. Nearby, children played with several "Big Trak" programmable toys which were set up on special roadways outside the computer rooms. Several of us have found that these toys (which behave similarly to a LOGO "turtle") are very well suited for teaching programming concepts to youngsters. (In case you wondered, Big Trak is a motorized device with a keyboard that accepts programs up to sixteen steps long. Once the program is entered, the user presses GO and watches the machine move along a path defined by the program.)

Next to an information booth, we had continuous showings of "Don't Bother Me, I'm Learning," the film on the use of computers in schools.

The smooth mixture of all these activities blended in with the leather work, crafts, music, food, and other activities of the Learning Faire to create a truly magical environment.

For your first activity, you may not want to start with something as big as participating in a major community event such as this one. Carefully assess your resources and people to see whether you can handle the planning and organization required. If you do help create a major community opportunity for people to access computers, you will reap the advantages of touching base with lots of people, quickly, and plenty of local media exposure.

Profile 3: A Word Processing Study Group

ComputerTown study groups offer people a chance to explore areas of specific interest. These might include word processing or other computer applications software, various types of games, or problems such as how to choose a personal or small business computer.

ComputerTown, Menlo Park offered its support and facilities to a study group on word processing, organized by David Warren. The study group had no designated teacher. A general consensus among members determined the course of study and exploration. The following report by David Warren reveals the kinds of issues study group participants might wish to consider:

> The purpose of the Menlo Park word processing study group was to help participants identify questions about word processing and find intelligent answers. The group began in August, 1981, and met once a month for the next four months. Most participants were interested in getting into word processing, but knew little about what was needed in the way of hardware and software. Group members were by and large interested in small-scale applications such as home or small business use.
>
> The group found resources in the community. Individuals who were already using microcomputers for word processing, as well as local computer store owners and personnel, seemed to welcome the opportunity to talk to the group about the many options available. Whereas it certainly is possible to talk with computer salespeople by simply visiting one's neighborhood computer stores, getting the same infor-

mation as part of a public group tends to soften the impression of being subjected to a sales pitch.

If you set up a similar group in another community, you will soon find numerous potential speakers. The computer store connections are as close as your yellow pages. Finding experienced word processing users is less straightforward, but in our experience, notices in the newspaper and contacts with computer store personnel turned up writers, editors, and others who were most happy to lend a hand. One contact led to another.

Speakers have talked about or demonstrated Apple, Vector Graphics and S-100 component hardware systems as well as the WordStar, Magic Wand, and Memorite III word processing programs. They have demonstrated NEC and Diablo printers, and talked about less expensive options.

Whether such a study group can or should be a stable and continuous activity is still an open question. Those who participate in such a group will eventually either become computer owners themselves, with no further reason to participate in an acquisition group, or possibly lose interest for one reason or another (they decide against purchasing a computer, for instance). In either case, you can expect the group to shrink. Unless some stable method is found to bring new people into the "front end," the activity will disappear, possibly leaving new generations of potential users out there in the community asking themselves, "Which computer should I buy? And which word processing programs?"

In this bureaucratic age, organizations sometimes spring up to fill a human need and then develop an independent "right to life" which is not always justified. The members of the word processing study group, having met for four months, found that they had fulfilled their original need to learn about word processing. What a great success! Why spoil it by turning the continuation of the group into a chore for its organizers?

Computing study groups, like the technology they study, are tools for people. They should be turned on and run as long as they are useful. When their job is done, turn them off! If we treat ComputerTown study groups this way, we will each feel free to start one whenever it is needed. We learn what we can from our neighbors and disband when our knowledge has been shared. The only legacy a ComputerTown study group need leave is people with some knowledge of computers.

Profile 4: A ComputerTown Conference

A well publicized ComputerTown conference is likely to bring out anywhere from two hundred to five hundred people eager for computer information. Be forewarned; a conference of this size is a lot of work. If managed well, it can be rewarding in terms of exposure and income for your ComputerTown.

Holly Anderson, founder of ComputerTown, Barrington, kicked off her computer literacy efforts with a conference. Here is Holly's account of her experiences:

Barrington, Illinois, March 13, 1982. Over 500 people attended a conference on the classroom and home uses of small computers at Barrington High School to hear noted author and educator LeRoy Finkel call for the establishment of an Illinois Computer-Using Educators (I-CUE) group.

"The Computer Challenge," as the event was billed, was designed to disseminate information about hardware, software, and services related to small computers. Although the conference was designed for classroom educators and school administrators, about a quarter of the workshop sessions were on topics of general interest.

Following Mr. Finkel's talk, each visitor attended as many as four one-hour sessions conducted by some of the Midwest's most knowledgeable experts in microcomputers for educational and personal use. Dr. Woody Sparrow of the Scarsborough (Ontario, Canada) Department of Education gave a very popular talk entitled, "An Apple a Day May Make Johnny Sick," considering the human side of classroom instruction with microcomputers. Other sessions covered topics ranging from computer music, graphics, and educational software to word processing and data base management. With over forty subjects offered, many people found selection difficult.

Response from conference attendees was very positive. Many ideas were exchanged, and we hope that one result of the conference might be the formation of an Illinois Computer-Using Educators organization. It is clear that the microcomputer is becoming an important part of the educational process in Northern Illinois.

Small computers such as the Apple II played an important part in the "behind the scenes" planning of the event. They were used to develop announcements, press releases, and letters; data base systems were used to keep track of volunteers and registrants; the conference budget and other financial tasks were also managed on computer.

The event was sponsored by ComputerTown, Barrington, a nonprofit community service organization formed to further the uses of computers in schools and homes. Helping ComputerTown organize the conference were two educational research and consulting groups: Project Micro-Ideas of Glenview and the Institute for Educational Research.

Even if your ComputerTown project is just starting out, try your hand at an event or two, using the hints in this section as a guide. Perhaps the members of your ComputerTown project feel comfortable with testing the water by putting on one event this year. Terrific! Plan it carefully, invite the community, then sit back and see what happens. Chances are, your ComputerTown event will achieve even more than its primary goal: to introduce the community to computers. Don't be surprised if you discover, as ComputerTown, Menlo Park volunteers did, that a well-attended event is a terrific magnet for prospective ComputerTown teachers, volunteers, students, and community resources.

4

Courses and Other Learning Activities

ComputerTown User Validation

Once word of your ComputerTown begins to get around locally, your hands may be full with newcomers eager to learn to use the machines. An average of eighty newcomers appeared at the Menlo Park Library test site each month. Kids were especially eager to get their hands on the new technology. Often they would rush in, sit breathlessly at a machine, and shout, "Hey, how do you work one of these things?"

It soon became clear that an organized procedure for introducing eager visitors to the rudiments of computer literacy was necessary. The process came to be called "Computer Validation." The notes that follow, based on the needs and experiences of ComputerTown, Menlo Park, are geared toward the special conditions of a library-based ComputerTown; however, they can easily be adapted to suit the validation needs of ComputerTown projects in most any setting.

The validation procedure began with filling out a validation form. The only requirement a person had to meet to be validated was that they had to show a current library card. The card could be from any library in the world.

The next step was learning to turn on the computer (in the following example, a Commodore PET). A cassette tape with a short loading time would be selected for loading. If the tape drive was of the external variety, it had to be connected to the back of the PET, and novices were cautioned to connect or disconnect the tape drive with care.

Next came the actual loading process. ComputerTown, Menlo Park trainers found it helpful at this point to explain the blinking "cursor" and the necessity of hitting the RETURN key. The users were then prompted by the computer to press the PLAY button on the tape drive.

The ensuing waiting process, although relatively short, often seems endless to youngsters eager to start slaying dragons and collecting treasures. To keep impatient minds focused, trainers would explain the sequence of steps the computer was performing, such as SEARCHING, FOUND, LOADING, and READY. Each step was displayed on the computer screen as the tape was searched and the program loaded.

Before instructing visitors to type RUN in response to the READY prompt, instructors stressed the importance of rewinding the tape, a necessary procedure which seemed to be one of the most difficult for new visitors to remember. Trainers reinforced this point by explaining that a tape stopped in the middle is subject to fingerprints, which often cause frustrating load errors.

After several minutes of play, first-time visitors stopped the program by hitting the RUN/STOP key, and cleared the screen by pressing the SHIFT and CLR/HOME keys. By learning to LIST the program, they could see that the game was still there even though the screen was cleared. To convince them even further, they were asked to type RUN again, and their game would appear. When they were ready to try a new game, they typed NEW to erase the program already in memory.

The final step was to LOAD a different tape without prompting, if possible. When this was accomplished, the visitors' library cards would be stamped with "ComputerTown, USA!." The visitors were then free to use the ComputerTown software and hardware on their own, whenever they wished.

Since validation was not limited to Menlo Park Library patrons, the project validated library cards from as far away as Canada, New York, and North Carolina. As a result, librarians from other libraries began to notice the ComputerTown validation stamps and to request information on how bring Computer-Town to their own facilities.

Each ComputerTown site may need some form of validation procedure for first-time users. The procedure is likely to vary according to available equipment, resources, and the computer experiences being offered. Feel free to modify what was done at Menlo Park to fit the needs of your site.

Software: Games

The kind of software your ComputerTown offers will have a direct impact on the physical environment, especially in the case of arcade games. If you decide to offer these games at your ComputerTown, keeping the computers with games in a separate location is one solution to the inevitable noise problem. This is especially important in a library setting. Scheduling a regular time for arcade games will also help. This offers people a chance to play the games, but avoids the disruptions that may occur when others nearby want to program, study, or do something that demands peace and quiet.

There is often a controversy about the educational value of computer games. Many commercial game and simulation software packages, however, contain a rich set of implicit learning activities for younger children. To use the software, the children have to master not only motor skills, but verbal, mathematical, visual, and problem-solving skills. Skill acquisition often occurs naturally, as the kids play the games. For example, the popularity of such fantasy games as Dungeons and Dragons nearly guarantees that several million children will be able to spell the words *Strength, Intelligence, Wisdom, Constitution, Charisma,* and *Dexterity.*

An educator can "mine" the commercial software packages for learning opportunities, and coordinate explicit learning tasks with the implicit learning content of the software. The software fosters periods of extended attention span on the part of the student; the educator guides the process so that learning is reinforced.

The crucial step on the part of the educator is to see the hidden learning potential in today's software. By looking beneath the "game" aspect of each software package, one can uncover any number of ways to facilitate learning. In some cases, this may require nothing more than encouraging a child to use paper and pencil to make a map of the maze or labyrinth being traversed. In other cases, especially for those packages that require coherent

There is often a controversy about the educational value of computer games. Many commercial game and simulation software packages, however, contain a rich set of implicit learning activities for
younger children. To use the software, the children have to
master not only motor skills, but verbal, mathematical, visual, and
problem-solving skills. Skill acquisition often occurs naturally, as the
kids play the games.

text responses from the player, perhaps nothing needs to be done. The child is already learning verb-noun relationships and the correct spelling of several hundred words.

The packages that best serve this dual role contain some common elements. One key component seems to be fantasy. Children are drawn to games and simulations that involve them in fantasy. While working with fantasy-based material, a child seems capable of absorbing large amounts of data, relationships, content, and structure.

A second important element appears to be graphics. Although a child will use a program without graphics (for example, any of the "Adventure" games from Adventure International or "ZORK" from Personal Software), children seem to prefer software with graphics. The images do not have to be sophisticated. Crude, low-resolution graphic displays are totally acceptable.

Hidden objects and treasures are another common element of the kids' most-liked programs. There are other aspects of the popular packages, as well. Multiple goals, conflict, sound and color, secret passages, puzzle solving, monsters, magic, and unexpected elements are especially noteworthy. From the software user's perspective, these key program elements come together in complex arrangements — elaborate logic puzzles to be unravelled, or simulated events that call upon strategy and planning skills. From the educator's perspective, the complexity affords ample opportunities for tying the software to specific principles and content.

Beginning Steps in Programming

Many visitors, both children and adults, will come to Computer-Town to learn about programming. Be prepared with sample programs for beginners to type into the computers. Short, single-sheet programs are just right for first-time users.

Scanning the different computer language books will help you locate programs that work well for the beginning programmer's first experience. Educational computing magazines, such as *Popular Computing*, will also have programs for simple activities such as making your own name flash across the screen. This may seem a bit simplistic to the accomplished programmer, but it is easy for newcomers to understand, brings quick gratification, and children especially seem to love it.

Here is a sample program recommended for beginners:

```
10 PRINT "their name";
20 GO TO 10
```

This program works equally well on PETs, TRS-80s, and Atari computers. Beginners can type their names or any combination of characters between the quote marks (' '). Make certain they put the semicolon (;) at the end of line 10. This tiny program works wonders for young and old alike. On PETs and Ataris, have them type groups of graphic characters between the quote marks to create "instant art."

Here is another program that beginners can try once they have mastered the two-line program shown above. Do not allow new users to try this second program until they are successful with the first one. The amount of precise typing required can be difficult for first-time users. When learners attempt this second program, work with them until they succeed.

PET	TRS-80	ATARI
10 PRINT "their name";	10 PRINT "their name";	10 PRINT "their name";
20 FOR I = 1 TO 200	20 FOR I = 1 TO 200	20 FOR I = 1 TO 200
30 NEXT I	30 NEXT I	30 NEXT I
40 PRINT "[CLR]";	40 CLS	40 PRINT "⟩"
50 FOR I = 1 TO 200	50 FOR I = 1 TO 200	50 FOR I = 1 TO 200
60 NEXT I	60 NEXT I	60 NEXT I
70 GO TO 10	70 GO TO 10	70 GO TO 10

These programs cause the characters that appear between the quote marks in line 10 to "flash" in the upper left corner of the screen. The only tricky part is to correctly type line 40 in each program. For the three computers, here is what the user must type at line 40:

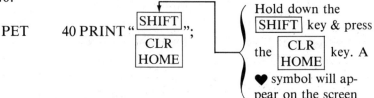

PET   40 PRINT "[SHIFT]/[CLR HOME]",;

Hold down the [SHIFT] key & press the [CLR HOME] key. A ♥ symbol will appear on the screen

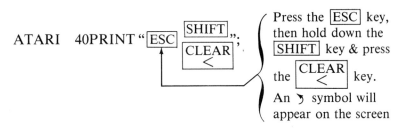

On the PET, a heart will appear between the quote marks. On the Atari, an arrow will appear. You can see why this program may be a bit complex for the first-time users. They type one character and see something different on the screen.

From this modest starting point, peple can be encouraged to work with self-teaching materials, to take a class or workshop on programming, or to explore on their own.

ComputerTown Courses

Once a week, or once a month, offer an open Family Night. The structure of Family Night can be very informal. It can include talking with people from the media, meeting with small groups of interested adults and/or kids, or just working with those who come in to use the computers. One or more project staff members should be on hand at the ComputerTown site for about two hours on a regularly scheduled basis to answer questions, give tips on how to use the machines, and provide a point of contact between the public and ComputerTown.

As time goes on, you might wish to offer introductory or assistance classes on specific software—how to use Visicalc, for example, or what a word processor can do for you.

For the purpose of this discussion, the term "course" will mean a series of class meetings with several students and a teacher. Courses are by no means mandatory for ComputerTown projects, but seem to be very popular whenever they are offered in a community. Here are some of the forms ComputerTown courses can take:

- Short-term ComputerTown courses that meet once a week for two or three weeks, with a total class time of three to nine hours.
- More extensive ComputerTown courses that last six to twelve weeks. Their schedules might coincide with local school calendars.
- Workshops on specific subjects that are held on one day, or over a single weekend.
- A study group supported by ComputerTown, but initiated and run by students learning together.
- Mentor programs and peer teaching that involve one-on-one instruction.

Sample Course Titles

ComputerTown, Menlo Park has offered courses entitled:

- "Computer Comfort" (for adults) or "Computer Play-shop" (for kids). Validation materials were presented in these class formats.
- "Computer Tool Use"
- "Introduction to BASIC"
- "Beginning, Novice, Intermediate, and/or Advanced BASIC"
- "Software Evaluation" (for adults) or "Computer Games" (for kids).

Curricula

Some ComputerTown teachers plan a structured curriculum and determine specific course objectives. Others spend part of the initial class meeting choosing what the group will study.

At ComputerTown, Menlo Park, for example, a group of adults ranging in age from 31 to 78 completed a series of classes designed to introduce them to a variety of microcomputers, increase each person's ability to communicate about the technology, and help develop software-evaluating skills.

The classes evaluated educational, business, recreational, and personal software packages using an eleven-point Software Evaluation Form, prepared especially for the class. The group rated each product according to ease of use, quality of program instructions, originality/creativity, error handling, educational value, written documentation, function, presentation/polish, use of graphics, challenge (for games), and overall value.

Experiment with different course offerings and workshops at your ComputerTown. Get people in existing courses to tell you what additional courses and workshops they would like to see. You can also find people willing to teach about specific subjects, and invite them to use your facilities for the courses.

Courseware: ComputerTown Scrapbooks

The fast pace of changes in personal computer technology make it difficult to provide timely information. The new consumer in this field has to dig through a bewildering array of machines, printed literature, jargon-laden advertising, technical stores, and computer programs to begin to get his or her initial questions answered. Textbooks are outdated almost as soon as they are printed. Several monthly magazines, with readerships exceeding 100,000, now target material for single computers.

The ComputerTown Scrapbooks provide one possible solution to the tasks of collecting and organizing current computer information and presenting that information to a diverse group of beginning users and consumers. At the Menlo Park Library site, the scrapbooks have been used both as resource and as text material by the general library patron. They were placed near the table where the computers were located. People were encouraged to browse through the scrapbooks, especially the one on "Computer Comfort," when they had questions or wanted information about the technology.

The scrapbooks provide a starting point for delivering information on microcomputers to interested individuals. Once the process is underway, they provide a general framework for updating and expanding the information base.

Each ComputerTown is encouraged to build its own books,

based on the needs of its patrons and locale and the availability of new information. The initial scrapbooks will evolve differently at each site. How these materials are updated, what is chosen for inclusion or exclusion, and what additional scrapbooks are to be started, will vary from site to site.

Using the Scrapbooks

Scrapbooks are designed to be "created" and "recreated" by their first users. For example, the first step is for someone to locate and make copies of articles and materials that fall into the scrapbook categories. In some cases, the scrapbook itself, once assembled, can serve as the "text" for introductory workshops or beginning courses in "Computer Comfort." The idea is that each site will use and adapt the scrapbook based on the way it chooses to present computers to beginners.

Sample Scrapbook Outline

At ComputerTown, USA!, five scrapbooks are under development for use within the library setting. The first, "Computer Comfort," presents a set of materials and course suggestions for people with no computer experience. "Computer Comfort" forms the core of the sample scrapbook presented at the end of this section.

The second scrapbook, called "Computer Awareness," follows "Computer Comfort." It addresses the needs of the individual with some computer knowledge, limited hands-on experience, and often, an expanded set of questions about the technology.

The third scrapbook focuses on a person's concerns for the computer as a tool. Called "Computer Tool Use," it provides a set of structured, hands-on opportunities for the person who wants to explore the use of a computer.

The fourth scrapbook, "Computer Programming for Beginners," explores programming and programming languages. The course emphasizes self-teaching, hands-on introductions to programming concepts for beginning users of the technology.

The final scrapbook outlines maintenance procedures for the site's computers. It is used by ComputerTown personnel and volunteers. This scrapbook, like the others, does not require a high level of sophistication.

The "Computer Comfort" scrapbook follows the structure outlined below. At your own location, use it as a guide and add or delete items as needed to provide the kind of beginning computer experience that you want to give to people.

Computer Comfort Scrapbook

I. Preface

II. Essential Vocabulary

III. Selected Readings

IV. Course Ideas

V. Site Resources

    A. Books (copy of all card catalog entries)

    B. Magazines

    C. Available Software

    D. A/V Materials

    E. Hands-on Materials (for use at computers)

VI. Suggested Bibliography

    A. Books (indicate which are on-site)

    B. Magazines (indicate which are on-site)

    C. Newsletters

VII. Local Resources

    A. People

    B. Places

    C. Classes

VIII. Other Resources/Information

Peer Teaching

As long as young people are not thrown into situations they are unequipped to handle, peer teaching is a marvelous way to spread computer literacy. At ComputerTown, Menlo Park, beginning children have successfully taught each other, their parents, and other adults. Beginning adults gained confidence by learning with their friends.

Who are "peers?" They can be people of the same approximate age, or of different ages with similar abilities. The peer teaching relationship works best when the teacher and learner are very close in know-how. By showing someone else how to follow a new procedure, the teacher learns a lot too.

If teacher and learner are agemates but diverse in their abilities, a peer teaching arrangement is less likely to work. The teacher may go too fast or choose material that is too advanced, and the learner is short-changed. Peer teaching seems to work best when the teacher is just a little ahead of the student.

ComputerTown Mentor Project

"She's learned everything they have on computers at school, and now she spends her evenings poring over manuals at home. But she needs some guidance and a chance to practice. How can we, as parents who don't know about computers, help her with the next steps?"

One solution is to form a ComputerTown Mentor Project to match self-motivated learners with more experienced computer hobbyists and professionals willing to share their knowledge.

How can you establish a mentor project through your ComputerTown? First, hold a ComputerTown meeting. Invite kids and adults who would like to find a mentor. Invite adults and older kids who would like to volunteer for the honor. Whoever coordinates the mentor project should be computer literate in order to evaluate the practical knowledge of potential mentors.

Your meeting agenda could go something like this:

- Invite people to come in and sit in a circle.
- Briefly introduce the ComputerTown mentor project.
- Start round-table introductions. Give your own name, occupation, and favorite computer-related topic, then invite others to do the same.

Peer teaching can be a great way to spread computer literacy. The peer teaching relationship works best when the teacher and learner are very close in know-how. By showing someone else how to follow a new procedure, the teacher learns a lot too.

- Have forms available for exchange of names and phone numbers. Also, offer "contract" forms like the example that follows this agenda.
- Open the meeting for discussion.
- Have two or three show-and-tell demonstrations available.
- Offer juice, coffee, tea, cookies, or whatever sounds tasty.
- Let informal associations form.

This should get your mentor project off to a good start. If only students in search of mentors show up, organize them into a mentor-finding committee. If only potential mentors appear, discuss the meaning of the mentor role, and compile a list of volunteer mentors to be distributed to schools in the community.

Sample Contract Form
ComputerTown, Anywhere Mentor Project

Mentor's Name _____

Address _____

Phone _____

I work/go to school at _____

I would like to teach _____

_____

_____

I have these computing resources available: _____

_____

I could be available at these times: _____

_____

Student's Name _____

Address _____

Phone _____

I work/go to school at _____

I would like to learn _____

In the brochure, "Mentorship for the Eighties," Kendra R. Bonnett* offers the following insights on the value of the mentor concept:

Today more than any other time in recent history, children have been cut off from the adult world. With legislation such as child labor laws limiting the employment of youth and protecting them from harsh working conditions, the greatest part of young people's time is spent in school in the company of their peers. Even in the home, children usually have their own space, separate from adults . . . Cut off as they are, young people today are often unprepared for the responsibilities facing them as adults. They are confused as to the relationship of their adolescent activities to their adult life, and at worst they are disaffected, alienated, and drawn toward delinquency.

During their growth to adulthood, young people require advisors and role models other than their peers, positions that in the past parents, relatives, teachers, and masters fulfilled. Today most of that responsibility falls to the teachers, who are not only ill-prepared to satisfy all of youths' needs, but also lack the time to give sufficient personal attention to each student. Although formal education can neither replace missing parental guidance nor change the economic and cultural features of society that have separated parent from child, it can perhaps suggest the means to ameliorate the ill effects. The school can serve as the medium for introducing, or rather reintroducing, the concept of mentorship.

For the youth the advantages of the mentorship relationship are clear. Mentorship has the potential to improve interpersonal skills and self-confidence, demonstrate the importance and application of classroom learning for solving real problems, and provide firsthand understanding of the nature of particular occupations and of adult working life. But the mentor benefits as well. An adult gains satisfaction from knowing she or he has accepted responsibility for the future by giving guidance to a person. It is the knowledge that something good has been put back into society.

---

*Reprinted with permission from "Mentorship for the Eighties," (November 1981) by Kendra R. Bonnett. Far West Laboratory, 1855 Folsom Street, San Francisco CA 94103.

5

ComputerTown Host
Institutions

Whether a ComputerTown is located in a public library, a senior center, a museum, school, or other public access site, the fundamental philosophy and approach to computer literacy remain constant. There are, however, certain characteristic needs and conditions which make each kind of host unique.

Computers at a Public Museum*

The public museum can be an ideal setting for hands-on exploration, structured demonstrations, and computer literacy classes. Although hundreds of children may take this opportunity to get close to a computer, their enthusiasm is likely to be well matched by adults, delighted to learn along with their kids in such a nonthreatening environment.

Museums typically offer three kinds of experience: the unattended exhibit, the guided demonstration, and the scheduled course in a typical classroom setting. Introducing microcomputers into any of the three situations offers the museum visitor a new form of interactive participation.

What hardware and software is appropriate for a museum exhibit? Nothing fancy; off-the-shelf hardware and software may

*From "Computers at a Public Museum" by Liza Loop. Reprinted with permission from THE ATARI CONNECTION,™ Volume 1, Number 2, Summer 1981, pp. 6-7.

seem to trifle dull if you have been experimenting with it for a year or so, but to the computer neophyte it's all new and exciting. A computer such as the Atari 400 with the Video Easel cartridge inserted and one joy stick, or a Texas Instruments 99/4A with an educational game cartridge will almost make a complete exhibit in itself. Add a copy of the instruction booklet protected by clear, self-adhesive shelf paper and you are in business. Whenever possible, cover switches and latches with Plexiglas panels so that visitors don't open or disconnect the equipment by mistake.

The Palo Alto Junior Museum in Palo Alto, California held a computer exhibit during March and April, 1981. Local retailers and manufacturers were able to lend systems for this short period of time. Commodore, Radio Shack, Atari, Texas Instruments, Hewlett Packard, and the local school district were all represented.

Software was loaded in the morning when the Junior Museum exhibit opened, and usually had to be reloaded several times during the day since many young visitors knew how to clear the computer's memory. Because of the delay of loading tapes, cartridge software seemed preferable when there were a lot of exhibit visitors. Each machine ran only one program for several days. This encouraged people to spend a little time at each computer, and then move on so that another visitor could have a turn.

Favorite software among the young museum visitors included Atari's "Video Easel" and "States and Capitals"; "Fire" and "Hurkle" from Creative Publications for the Radio Shack TRS-80; and "Lemonade Stand" for the Commodore PET. Also popular were the disk-based math games developed by Science Research Associates. Video games such as "Space Invaders" and "Star Raiders" were specifically absent from the exhibit. They are so engrossing for some visitors that the museum would not have been able to handle the competition for machines.

Visitors with some computer experience delighted in clearing out the tape-based software and writing their own small BASIC programs. Although this activity had not been included in the original plan, it worked rather well and soon became the custom, with visitors teaching each other how to program the computers.

What do people learn in a free access computer exhibit at a public museum, or any other public access setting? First, people discover that computers don't bite — they don't explode and spit fire as in the science fiction portrayals, and they don't attempt to take control of the world or order the hapless beginner around.

Second, people begin to see the versatility of computer technology. By experiencing games, simulations, and rudimentary BASIC programming, adult visitors to the Junior Museum began to formulate their own answers to the question, "How could I use a computer?"

Third, by actually pressing keys and operating the machines themselves, people gain practical knowledge of how to use a computer. Once a minimal threshold of confidence and interest is crossed, many people choose to take short classes in computer programming or the use of application software or computer-assisted instruction.

Fourth, in every real computer environment, people see some examples of machine failure and many examples of apparent machine failure which usually turn out to be user generated. Visitors discover that everyone makes mistakes, even computer experts; that machines are usually reliable but not infallible; and that each of us can learn to use computers if we keep an exploratory attitude and don't quit.

The following museums are among the many which incorporate microcomputer technology into their exhibits:

- Boston Children's Museum, Museum Wharf, Boston, Massachusetts (617) 426-6500; 426-8855
- Capital Children's Museum, 800 3rd Street, N.E., Washington, D.C. (202) 543-8600
- Coyote Point Museum, Coyote Point Dr., San Mateo, California (415) 573-2595
- The Franklin Institute, 20th & Benjamin Franklin Parkway, Philadelphia, Pennsylvania (215) 448-1000
- Lawrence Hall of Science, Centennial Dr., Berkeley, California (415) 513-2415
- Oregon Museum of Science and Industry, 4015 S.W. Canyon Rd., Portland, Oregon (503) 222-2828
- Pacific Science Center, 200 2nd North, Seattle, Washington (206) 625-9333
- Sesame Place, 100 Sesame Rd., Langhorne, Pennsylvania (215) 757-1100

Libraries

If a public library is your ComputerTown host, take pains to develop a good rapport with members of the library staff. While not all will take an active role in ComputerTown, the jobs and working environments of everyone on the library staff will be affected in some way. Pay close attention to their feedback and suggestions.

You may arrange to bring in a ComputerTown staff member to monitor the project during library hours, or you may agree to appoint one member of the existing library staff. Whatever the arrangement, everyone involved must recognize that monitoring ComputerTown activities in the library is a considerable amount of work. It should not be added nonchalantly to an already full working schedule.

Micros in the Menlo Park Library—An Assessment

When microcomputers had been in the Menlo Park Public Library for nearly two years, ComputerTown evaluators sat down with two members of the library staff who had been on the site while the computers were in use. The object of the meeting was to record their candid comments about microcomputers in the library setting. Their observations fell into several generic categories. The following notes cover some concerns and comments expressed by the librarians, and the ComputerTown staff's and librarians' suggestions for improvement.

Software

Problems/Concerns

- Game tapes were a problem. They increased the noise and physical activity in the library.
- A separate room is needed if game tapes are to continue to be used.
- Tape circulation was a problem due to limited staff.

- The library staff needed more training in the use of a cassette-based software, especially in troubleshooting bad tapes.

Possible Solutions

- Discuss candidly with the library staff whether games software is to be part of the software collection. If not, recommend other kinds of software products. ComputerTown is not a mandate to turn a library into an arcade parlor.
- Devise a system for routine computer repairs.
- Replace worn tapes and tape players.
- Implement a formal circulation system for software and, if applicable, for hardware units.
- Train and periodically retrain library staff in the use of computers and software.

Space

Problems/Concerns

- The initial location for computers, the children's section, was too small for the number of computers that were installed.
- The computers were too near the only available study area.
- The noise levels around the computers were not appropriate for that section of the library.

Possible Solutions

- Limit the number of computers in that part of the library.
- Limit the number of kids per computer to minimize the noise levels.
- If possible, use a separate room for computers.
- Fit the computers into the library environment and prevailing usage patterns.

- In the future, library designers need to look at the appropriate integration of information technologies alongside traditional library functions.

Increased Library Usage

Problems/Concerns

- When word got out that computers were available, after-school crowds became a problem.
- Working parents were using the library as a free, de facto childcare service.
- The extra patron load and competition for computers caused some discipline problems.

Possible Solutions

- Schedule computer usage so that patrons know several days in advance when they are to be in the library for their turn with the equipment.
- Limit usage per patron to some fixed amount of time per week.
- Contact the local schools and ask them to alert parents regarding your attitudes toward de facto childcare situations.
- To handle patrons who foster discipline problems, take away or limit their privilege of using the computers.

Success

Problems/Concerns

- Concern was expressed that the project be successful in terms of the goals and objectives of a library.
- The need to integrate computers into regular services was cited.

- More print product support to go with the computers was needed.
- It was felt that success could not be achieved without additional staffing.

Possible Solutions

- Take care to integrate computers into existing services from the outset of the project.
- Get a clear definition of the level of service the organization wishes to provide.
- Have the organization and its staff who will deal with computers state what they wish to achieve by putting computers at their location.
- Provide a list of available print products that can support the project.
- Have a monitor from the ComputerTown staff available to answer questions, supervise activities, and handle technical problems during the early project stages.
- Determine whether there is a need for additional staff.
- Don't let the project start off as a burden to a few already overworked individuals.
- Work closely with the organization's staff to met their goals and support their definitions of what constitutes a successful project.

Planting New ComputerTowns

Judging from ComputerTown experiences in California, some of your events and activities will plant ComputerTown seeds in neighboring areas. Don't be surprised if people you have been working with decide to strike out on a ComputerTown project of their own. During this period of explosive growth in computing, there is a corresponding need for more public access computer literacy projects. ComputerTown International encourages the formation of autonomous computer literacy projects so long as there are people anxious to learn. The ComputerTown International network will keep communication lines open between the projects.

Many existing organizations are particularly fertile soil for ComputerTowns. Senior centers, Boys' and Girls' Clubs, YM/YWCAs, day care centers, centers for the mentally and physically handicapped, and other community facilities are ideal. Groups such as the American Association of University Women, the League of Women Voters, and various service clubs in your community might also be open to sponsoring ComputerTowns. Since many are linked through national organizations, word of one chapter's computer literacy activities will likely spread through those channels, and still more ComputerTowns will emerge.

Several institutions in the Menlo Park area hosted ComputerTown workshops and went on to develop ComputerTown projects of their own. The following notes describe what happened.

Computers at the Senior Center

Before it became a computer literacy project in its own right, Menlo Park's Little House Senior Center was the site of an event presented by ComputerTown, USA! ComputerTown staff brought computers to the lunch room of the center during the noon hour. About 120 seniors attended lunch that day, and as they finished eating, they began to come forward to ask questions and use the machines. The seniors were eager to learn and explore what the computers could do for them. Inquiries went all the way from, "What are these things?" to "How can I use this to monitor my real estate and financial portfolio transactions?" People were interested in art, music, writing, and general home management tasks that could be assisted by microcomputers.

Matt Lehmann, an active member of Little House, decided to develop a full-fledged ComputerTown at the senior center. The Little House project began with one "seed computer" on loan from ComputerTown, USA! Palo Alto, California's "Computer Tutors" program later donated a new set of time-sharing terminals to the project, purchased with the aid of a local foundation.

"The home computer is becoming so much a part of our daily life that a comfortable acquaintance with this new appliance is essential for everyone," Matt says. "Although much has been accomplished in making the younger members of society comfortable with computers and their use, the elder citizen has been neglected. In an effort to rectify this error, Little House has initiated a class in computer demystification and use. This makes it possible for the seniors to study and work in a familiar and comfortable noncompetitive atmosphere. They study with people in their own age group, so that do not feel that they will look foolish in trying to absorb some of the complexities of computer language."

Computers at the Boys' Club

In January, 1981, ComputerTown, USA! held an event at the Herbert Hoover Boys' Club in Menlo Park, California. During the day more than forty kids, several parents, a few interested adults, and a news reporter got their hands on the computers. The staff spent a busy two hours providing information, loading software, working with the kids, and answering the reporter's inquiries. As they packed to leave, one of the girls who attended the event typed the following message on the computer screen:

BRING ME ONE FOR CHRISTMAS!

An enthusiastic article in the local paper and another in *Recreational Computing* magazine combined with word of mouth to bring a flood of community response. So, with the help of a Commodore computer donated by Bob Albrecht, the Boys' Club began an ongoing computer science training program. "Since then, the computer project has been in full swing and great demand," reports Boys' Club President Margo Ritter. At present, the club has three computers (an Atari, a PET, and a TRS-80), with open access hours from 4:00 to 8:00 p.m. daily. Plans are in the making for the building of a special computer room in the club.

Pelton Steward, who facilitates the project, is introducing computers to Boys' Clubs all around the area — including the San Francisco Boys' Club, which played a supportive role in his own formative years. A special "traveling computer" is devoted to the task.

Several fundamental differences between the projects

The ComputerTown School Outreach Project provides the schools with expertise in teaching computer literacy and knowledge about equipment, software, and key people in the field. Schools, in turn, can help ComputerTown reach more members of the community.

described above and the Menlo Park Library ComputerTown test site are worthy of note.

- The Herbert Hoover Memorial Boys' Club and the Little House Senior Center focused on a narrowly defined user base. A library must serve a great number of people with diverse interests and needs. Its primary purpose is to provide information, whereas these other facilities provide educational or vocational opportunities and activities.
- In an activity-oriented setting, there may be synergy between the ComputerTown and other activities. At the Little House Senior Center, for example, the shop classes built cabinets for the machines. This kind of opportunity is not available at a site like the library.
- The Herbert Hoover Boys' Club and the Little House Senior Center each had one key person who was committed to seeing the project happen. Computers were introduced to the Menlo Park Library from an outside source; no member of the library staff had initiated the project.
- Finally, these sites set aside a particular area for the computers. The library computers were placed within the existing physical arrangements.

After conducting a few introductory events and seeding one or two computers, the role of ComputerTown, USA! diminished, leaving the Boys' Club and the Little House Senior Center to thrive by themselves. These projects were especially successful in that they were self-starting, self-generating, and did not require a great deal of outside support. Interestingly enough, none of these projects had a highly technical volunteer on staff.

ComputerTown School Outreach Project

Schools at the elementary, secondary, college, and continuing education levels wrote the majority of letters requesting information from ComputerTown, USA!. But school classrooms rarely provide "public access" in the same way that libraries, museums, community centers, and Boys' Clubs do. The purpose of the ComputerTown School Outreach Project was to create a synergy between the schools' need for expertise in the computer field to enhance their curricular program and ComputerTown's mandate to improve computer access and knowledge for the general population. Through developing the School Outreach Project, ComputerTown hoped to benefit both the schools and their surrounding communities.

The School Outreach Project is quite simple. The ComputerTown project has expertise in teaching computer literacy and setting up successful computer literacy programs as well as knowledge about equipment, software, and key people in the field. The ComputerTown staff can advise schools on setting up their own classroom-based computer literacy projects. The school can, in turn, help ComputerTown reach more members of the community. The school can make any arrangement it chooses to promote computer literacy outside the classroom. No effort is considered too small. One Saturday per semester might be set aside for computer students to teach their family, friends, and neighbors the same material they have been learning in class.

Schools open to more public involvement have a number of additional options. For instance, the school's computer equipment might be made available to scouting and other youth groups after school hours. The students could arrange with Rotary or other business groups to give demonstrations. Visiting programs could be arranged with schools that do not yet have computer literacy projects. Students could be assigned to teach two other people who would not normally have had access to this equipment for two or three hours per semester. Teachers might be encouraged to give after-school classes sponsored by the city's adult or continuing education programs or the recreation department. In some districts, arrangements might be made to move the school's computers to a nearby public library for use during weekends and vacation periods.

Non-Facility Centered ComputerTown Groups

So far, we have discussed ComputerTown activities which are associated with institutions. But the ComputerTown spirit can work just as well in your neighborhood or at your house—especially as the number of personal computers grows. You will need the same key ingredients necessary for any ComputerTown—a person with know-how who is ready to share, some others who want to learn, and one computer. You can even start without a computer and set your first goal to raise enough money to buy one.

Neighborhood Computer Clubs

If the idea of a neighborhood ComputerTown group sounds like it would suit your needs, here is a list of suggestions:

- Set up a structure for your neighborhood group's first goal: this might be to obtain a computer and software. Discuss the details, set up a strategy, and then go to it! Be sure to look into the possibility of a discount from the dealer for a "buying pool," and before you buy the computer of your choice, be sure to determine each member's share of expense and access to the new computer.

- The same considerations go for software as well as the computer. Your neighborhood group will need to divide the software cost and circulation among its members. You might even consider a "rental-based" system of software circulation.

- To finance your neighborhood computer club, you might want to offer a ComputerTown neighborhood garage sale—or even several of them, simultaneously. When you advertise the day on flyers, newspaper announcements, and so forth, you will also be letting the public know about your plans for a neighborhood ComputerTown. With an approach like this, you can earn funds and gain new neighborhood participants at the same time.

- If your club would rather skip the equipment issue altogether, field trips are another way to increase your computer literacy and have a lot of family fun. You can visit the bank, the grocery store, the newspaper, the police station, and, of course, your local computer store, to name

Not all ComputerTowns are associated with institutions. They can
work just as well in your neighborhood or at your house—especially
as the number of personal computers grows. You will need the
same key ingredients—a person with know-how who is ready to
share, others who will want to learn, and one computer.

ComputerTown is grassroots, informal learning. No matter where your project's base of operations might be, no matter how structured or easygoing its activities, the all-important ingredient that really makes a ComputerTown is "people helping people learn about computers."

just a few. Call ahead to each site and ask if a representative can meet with you to explain how computers are used there. These trips will make great school reports for kids!

• The goals of your group will of course be determined by the individuals who comprise it, but they will presumably be something along the lines of sharing ideas, experience, and knowledge about computers. A loose, relaxed structure is most fitting for your neighborhood Computer-Town. Meetings can take place once a week (less often if you choose) at the house of whichever member is currently keeping the computer and software (if your group has any). Activities can include informal presentations, lectures, discussions, brainstorming sessions, or problem solving get-togethers.

• The neighborhood ComputerTown organizers should be responsible for the guidance and direction of the group as a whole. They should consider how to publicize the group's existence and activities, how to handle organizational details, and either be able to take on teaching responsibilities themselves, or have ready access to someone who will.

• The members' responsibilities would include a democratic participation in major decisions, helping to determine the group's direction and objectives, and taking a personal responsibility to see that their own goals are realized through the group's activities.

Users' Groups

A users' group is an association of people who share a common interest in a specific piece of technology. Also called hobby clubs, such organizations usually focus on the equipment of particular manufacturer—Digital Equipment Corporation, or Sinclair, for example. Sometimes they are oriented toward software, perhaps the CPM operating system or LOGO language. As a users' group grows, it may develop subsections, called SIGs (special interest groups).

When you start your ComputerTown, be sure to visit the

users' groups nearby and enlist their help. Users' group members are among your richest sources of information and know-how. Most hobbyists are eager to explain their latest computer gadget, and will talk well into the night to any interested listener. Many people will be happy to bring their own equipment to the events you plan.

Remember that ComputerTown is grassroots, informal learning. No matter where your project's base of operations might be, no matter how structured or easygoing its activities, the all-important ingredient that really makes a ComputerTown is "people helping people learn about computers."

6

Creating a Formal Organization

Since each local ComputerTown is autonomous, there are no limits to the variety of organizational structures that can develop. Some projects have begun as isolated events, exhibits, demonstrations, workshops, and playdays that were so popular that a regular schedule developed. For convenience, projects have joined with existing institutions that already had meeting rooms, equipment storage, and administrative facilities. Libraries, museums, youth clubs, schools, and community centers around the world are adopting computer literacy projects. Computing organizations such as hobby clubs and professional societies often add the ComputerTown concept of public education to their other activities. Alternatively, the governing boards of many public and private organizations are choosing to offer computing as an integral part of their regularly supported services.

The organization of a ComputerTown reflects the needs of the people who plan and present the activities. Some Computer-Towns have no formal structure. They just seem to happen. This was true of the original ComputerTown in Menlo Park. However, when a ComputerTown exists within a host nonprofit organization such as a library, museum, school, or civic club, it is normal to take on the host's way of doing things. The same is true if the host is a "for profit" company—a store or manufacturer, for example—which is supporting the ComputerTown as a public service gesture. Of course, your ComputerTown might be completely independent, functioning as an association of individuals or a nonprofit corporation.

However you choose to set up your ComputerTown, don't

wait for it to be perfect. Just start. Your organizational needs will make themselves known as you explore and experiment with the ComputerTown experience in your own particular setting.

ComputerTown Charters

Whether a ComputerTown exists independently or under the umbrella of another institution, a concise statement of the project's purpose and activities will keep communication open between volunteers, visitors, and the community. The sample ComputerTown Charter below might be appropriate for an independent ComputerTown. It might also work if you are affiliated with another loosely organized group. However, many existing organizations already have regulations under which the ComputerTown project may fall. To avoid potential conflict, check this out thoroughly. The sample charter may be copied or modified to describe the purpose and function of any community-based ComputerTown project. Be sure to have a lawyer review your charter to ensure that it is consistent with local, state, and national laws.

Sample Charter: ComputerTown, Anywhere

1. Purpose

ComputerTown, Anywhere is a voluntary association of individuals who come together from time to time for educational and social purposes. The specific interests of ComputerTown, Anywhere members are:

- To become "computer literate" by learning to use and to program computers.
- To explore the varied uses of computers and their impact on society.
- To provide public access to computers, free of charge, and to help other interested individuals become computer literate.

2. Activities

ComputerTown, Anywhere may engage in, but is not limited to, the following activities:

- Hold meetings.
- Conducting classes.
- Disseminating information through the publication of a newsletter or obtaining coverage in local news media.
- Maintaining a library of printed and electronic material for use by members and the public.
- Maintaining a public access computer facility.
- Raising funds to cover operating expenses and to purchase equipment.
- Accepting donations of money, equipment, and professional services to further the project's activities and services.
- Arranging the purchase of goods and/or services in order to obtain volume discounts for members.

3. Membership

Membership in ComputerTown, Anywhere is open to any individual, adult or child, who shares the interests stated in this charter and would like to participate in ComputerTown, Anywhere's activities.

No membership fee may be assessed to cover general expenses incurred by ComputerTown, Anywhere. However, specific activities may require a fee from each participant sufficient to defray the costs of that activity. No funds may be collected or distributed, purchases made, or charges incurred for the benefit of any individual member. ComputerTown, Anywhere funds may not be distributed for the personal profit or gain of any private individual.

Membership is not available to businesses or other groups. If such organizations wish to be informed of ComputerTown, Anywhere's activities, at least one individual from that group must become a member of ComputerTown, Anywhere. This person may then act as liaison for his or her organization.

Businesses or other commercial organizations may become sponsors of ComputerTown, Anywhere. Sponsors may donate goods or services to the ComputerTown, Anywhere membership organization in return for promotional consideration. A sponsoring organization, however, may not require any further obligation from the ComputerTown group as a whole or its individual members.

Should ComputerTown, Anywhere dissolve or discontinue activities, any assets held by the organization will be sold and the proceeds distributed equally among its current members, or donated to a nonprofit organization.

Be sure to deal with three potential legal issues in your charter:

- Who or what legal entity owns any assets (cash, equipment, books, software, or other supplies) which may be donated to or earned by your project?
- Who will carry liability insurance to protect your staff, volunteers, and the public in the event of an accident?
- What, if any, are the tax consequences of the organization and its activities?

Consult with your accountants and attorneys on these issues.

Funding

There are many ways to fund your ComputerTown. Three of the most common funding strategies are through cost-recovering activities, grants, or the host institution's operating budget.

Cost-Recovery Funding

A cost-recovery system involves a charge to each participant for activities and services provided by ComputerTown. Some events are specifically designed as fundraisers. Other activities, such as classes or workshops, usually set prices just high enough to cover expenses. This helps fulfill the ComputerTown ideal of low-cost or free public access to computing.

Speakers and teachers donate their services; the meeting room is hopefully free; equipment is loaned. Attendees are asked for a donation at the door, and a good time is had by all. ComputerTown puts the money in the bank to be spent on equipment, software, salaries, supplies, and whatever it takes to promote computer literacy.

Grant Funding Strategy

Acquiring money from funding agencies involves three basic tasks. First, research and identify likely funding sources; second, plan an effective funding strategy for your needs; third, write the proposal.

Developing a funding strategy for your organization requires, first of all, substantial research and planning. The success of your request will depend on how well the objectives are defined. Your terms should be understandable, meaningful, and realistic. What does your organization need to effectively implement your project, and why? Assessing your project in this way will enable you to find a funding agency with similar interests, and to develop your formal proposal based on your research.

Thorough research into funding agencies will help narrow the field to one or two appropriate target agencies. The three types of funding sources to consider are government agency grants, foundation grants, and business or industry grants. Several criteria should be used to select the target agencies. You can include items such as the agencies' geographical limitations, funding priorities or special fields of interest, average size of grants, types of grants (e.g., seed money, operating support, or matching funds), and the agencies' funding cycles.

Information on the various grant-making agencies can usually be found in a large public library. Ask the reference librarian for help in locating them. The following books contain useful information:

For governmental programs:

- *Catalog of Federal Domestic Assistance* (dubbed the Sears-Roebuck of government grants).

- *United States Government Manual* (emphasizes activities of various agencies and addresses for requesting grant information).
- *Federal Register* (includes announcements of new grant programs; published daily).

For foundation research:

- *The Foundation Directory* (gives basic information on 2,818 foundations).
- *The Foundation Grants Index* (indexed by state, foundation name, and subject).
- *The Foundation Center National Data Book* (identifies smaller foundations not included in the above directories).
- *Foundation Center Source Book Profiles* (detailed information on 500 major foundations and listings of past grant recipients).

For business or industry research:

- *Corporate Foundation Profiles* (details 500 corporations and can be accessed by subject, type of support, and geographical region).

The Foundation Directory, Foundation Grants Index, and the *Federal Register* are available on-line through DIALOG, a computerized information retrieval system available in some libraries.

Several foundations and corporations are interested in supporting projects that focus on education and technology. Read through the *Corporate Foundation Profiles* and the *Foundation Center Source Book Profiles*. Both these resources will give detailed information on the major foundations and corporations, and their funding priorities. Check the various foundations and corporations in your state and area. Often, their gifts are restricted geographically and you may have the advantage if they are located in your vicinity.

Other useful resources for researching foundations and corporations include:

- Lilly Endowment
- L.J. Skaggs
- Alfred P. Sloan
- Bell and Howell
- Zellerbach Family Fund
- Charles F. Kettering
- Dolfinger-McMahon
- Levi Strauss
- Tandy Corporation
- Exxon Education Foundation
- Control Data Corporation
- IBM Corporation
- Apple Foundation
- Atari Institute
- W.K. Kellogg Foundation
- Spencer Foundation
- Rockefeller Family Fund

Begin by looking up these foundations in the various directories. Write for their proposal guidelines, and formulate your presentation. There are other foundations that will fund educational projects—this list is not exhaustive. With thorough research, you may find a private endowment in your area to help you.

Additional resources and ideas for funding sources include:

- *Grant Money and How to Get It: A Handbook for Librarians*, by Richard W. Boss.
- *Funding Report for Microcomputers*, a free booklet published by Bell & Howell.
- *Federal Funding Guide and Proposal Development Handbook for Educators*, published by Radio Shack.

• "Funding Sources for Microcomputers," in *Instructional Innovator*, September, 1980.

At least three popular microcomputer manufacturers have established grant programs. Radio Shack, a division of Tandy Corporation, committed $500,000 worth of TRS-80 computer equipment to a grant program designed to encourage and support the successful application of microcomputer technology in U.S. education institutions. The Tandy TRS-80 Educational Grants Program awards TRS-80 hardware, software, courseware, and related projects to individuals or nonprofit educational institutions whose proposals are selected as providing the greatest benefit to the American educational community. An impartial Educational Grants Review Board has been established to review submitted proposals and make recommendations for equipment allocations. An information packet containing a cover letter, TRS-80 brochure, catalog, submission information, and a proposal cover sheet will be forwarded on request. For more information contact Tandy TRS-80 Educational Grants Program, Radio Shack Education Division, 400 Tandy Atrium, Forth Worth, TX 76102.

The Atari Institute for Educational Action Research fosters innovative yet practical uses of personal computers in education. The Institute provides grants of Atari computer products and/or cash stipends to selected institutions, individuals, or organizations able to develop and promulgate new uses for computers in education — whether in established institutions, community programs, or in the home. Applicants are requested to present a written abstract of their projects and interests, focusing on objectives, implementation, and especially, proposed evaluation and dissemination of results. For further details on preparing an Atari Grant Proposal, write to Ted M. Kahn, Executive Director, Atari Institute, 1265 Borregas Ave., P.O. Box 427, Sunnyvale, CA 94086.

The Foundation for the Advancement of Computer-Aided Education (formerly the Apple Education Foundation) offers grants to organizations and individuals for projects aimed at creating innovative methods of learning through low-cost technology. An informative brochure may be obtained by writing to the Foundation at 20863 Stevens Creek Blvd., Bldg. B-2, Suite A-1, Cupertino CA, 95014.

During the initial research and planning stages of your proposal, several other tasks should be taken into consideration. One is to establish a base of community support. Statistics, endorsements, and quotes will need to be included in your proposal. Concrete examples and quantified assessments of need will help justify your project. Developing contacts and cultivating the support of your board of directors or trustees is also important.

Writing the Proposal

Having completed your research and selected a target funding agency, you are ready to start the application procedure. Some agencies have specific procedures, forms, or deadlines. Send a letter to the agency or foundation to inquire about these procedures and to establish your intentions. This initial contact letter should be brief, no longer than two pages. Identify your organization as a potential applicant, describing succinctly your needs, anticipated accomplishments and impacts, and the nature, time frame, and total dollar amount of your proposed program. Using the information gained through your research, address the letter to the foundation manager or principal officer, not "to whom it may concern."

In a few weeks, the foundation or agency will probably inform your organization of any decisions they may have made. The letter may politely state that your project does not conform to their current priorities, or it may ask you to submit a longer, more formal proposal. The specific agency to which you have applied may have its own form or guidelines; however, all proposals generally follow the same format and require the same general information. The organizational assessment and planning you have done during the research phase provides an efficient outline for this next step. Your formal proposal should include the following components: summary, introduction, needs assessment, goals/objectives, methodology, evaluation, future funding, budget, and attachment. Let's take a look at them one by one.

Summary

The summary is usually the first, and sometimes the only, part read by the foundation officer, and it should be gripping. A clear and concise summary should:

- Identify the applicant and include a phrase or two about the applicant's credibility.
- Include the reason for the request and the objectives to be met through this funding.
- Briefly describe the activities that will be conducted to accomplish the objectives.
- Specify the total cost of the project, and the amount requested in the proposal.

Introduction

The introduction establishes your organization's qualifications or credibility. It might include a brief history of your organization, prior and current activities, accomplishments and impact, size and characteristics of your clientele, quotes or letters of support, important publications, and other relevant information.

Needs Assessment

The needs assessment section focuses on some need or problem of your clientele and should clearly relate to your ComputerTown's goals and objectives. Supporting evidence such as statistics, authoritative statements, and clients' requests is instrumental in justifying your needs.

Goals and Objectives

The most difficult aspect of proposal writing is differentiating between goals/objectives and methodology. Objectives of your proposed program are the outcome of the activities and not the activities or methods themselves. Program objectives should define in numerical terms who and how many will be served by your project, what you hope to accomplish in what time frame, and how you plan to measure your success.

Methodology

Once needs and objectives have been made clear, the next step is to describe the methods or activities that will be used to achieve the desired results. Activities should be clearly defined and justifiable. The sequence of proposed activities, the project's proposed staffing, and the intended clientele should be described. The scope of activities should be reasonably attainable within the allotted time.

Evaluation

This section describes methods that will be used to evaluate your program's effectiveness. It presents a plan for determining the degree to which the objectives are met and the assessment methods to be followed. The plan should cover the process of data collection and analysis, define evaluation criteria, and describe the production of evaluation reports.

Funding from the Host Institution and Other Possibilities

Writing grants for your computer projects can be both rewarding and time consuming. When time is a critical factor, alternatives to grant writing can produce more immediate results. The easiest way to obtain funding is to ask your "Town Hall" host institution to take ComputerTown under its budgetary wing. The host institution's managerial staff will be able to fill you in on any required procedures.

Creating alternative sources of support can be as easy as approaching some of the regular library users, members of your library commission or board of trustees, and teachers in your local school district. They can refer you to a vast network of potential support. Contact your state library association to find out about your state's Library Services and Construction Act. Several libraries have received LSCA funds to set up computer literacy projects.

Support may come from corporations in your area willing to donate equipment or funds in exchange for services which would benefit their employees. Managers of local computer stores may donate equipment if it can be justified in terms of public relations and generation of potential business. Members of local computer user groups may be willing to volunteer equipment, software, or teaching support for special events. Many libraries and museums have "Friends" groups which may provide a ready source of funds for furniture or equipment.

Fundraising with the specific objective of purchasing a computer can include a variety of activities. Portions of the proceeds from a book fair sale can be appropriated toward the purchase of a microcomputer. A "fun run" can be staged as part of your activities during National Library Week.

Your project can be sustained by fees from introductory classes on microcomputers. You may also decide to install a coin operating device in order to "rent" time on your computer. The recreation department in your city could start a computer club and use your facilities for a modest charge. Local schools may be interested in holding computer literacy classes in the public library, paying for the services rather than purchasing several microcomputers for the school.

You might also consider approaching your project from a unique angle. Why not set up a microcomputer center for senior citizens, provide reading literacy programs via microcomputer, or offer special access to computers for deaf or handicapped persons? Providing services for specific groups will often make funding easier, since you can approach foundations that specialize in funding programs for certain target organizations.

Innovative funding strategies can take many different forms. Let your creativity soar!

7

Conclusion

Now that you have reached the end of this book, we trust that you are inspired to start your own ComputerTown. If you live in an area where there are no computer literacy activities, perhaps you will be the person to start a few. If you are already involved in computer literacy projects, you may have already invented a new approach or two. If you are part of a techno-ghetto, you might have neighbors who share your interests and dreams. If you once thought that the computer age was only for younger people, perhaps now you will reconsider.

ComputerTown is a cultural movement we invite you to join. What you decide to do is, of course, up to you. By the time you read this document, many new ComputerTown activities will have taken place and a number of new ComputerTown sites will have formed. The invitation is for you to become part of this exciting and rewarding adventure in bringing computers to the public.

In the future—when we, our children, and their children use computers regularly—perhaps there will be no need for ComputerTowns. Right now, though, people need information and access to microcomputers. ComputerTowns can assist by placing microcomputers in public places.

The ComputerTowns we build today will help us cope with the accelerating changes brought on by the use of the technology. ComputerTowns are investments in our own future. So, make your ComputerTown strong and functional. Use our models and suggestions, or invent your own expression of the concept. Remember: in your community, ComputerTown is whatever you declare it to be. Bring forth your ComputerTown by telling the world that you exist and that you are ready to be the person who is "bringing computer literacy to your community."

A

Handling
ComputerTown
Resources

An important part of any ComputerTown is the organization of resources and services: physical environment, hardware, software, printed materials, people, classes, workshops, special programs, and of course, funding. This section will serve as a checklist of the detailed aspects of conducting a ComputerTown. It will cover, among other topics, the physical space, maintenance, software storage, use of print materials, inventory, troubleshooting, and security.

The Physical Arrangement

Once your ComputerTown begins to take root in its public access "Town Hall" facility, it is a good idea to design a physical arrangement to serve the needs of ComputerTown patrons and to accommodate those who may visit the host institution for other reasons. In the Menlo Park library, for instance, other activities were sometimes disrupted by exuberant youngsters at the terminals. Four or five computers in a very small space resulted in a lot of close physical contact, including occasional fights.

Facilitators determined that the noise and rowdiness could be eased by rearranging the environment. It was decided that each computer should have as much surrounding space as possible. No more than two computers should be used for playing games. Two computers were moved into the adult library section, and children unattended by a parent were discouraged from using these machines.

The Little House Senior Citizens' Center in Menlo Park experienced similar noise and congestion in its ComputerTown site. The problem was eased when a special area was designated for computer use, with some individually designed enclosures to house the equipment.

Don't be reluctant to look at new ways to locate and house the computers. For example, Figure 1 shows proposed design for a microcomputer installation that will conserve space and limit noise. This design includes a partition, 6 to 7 feet high, made of acoustical tiles or other materials, isolating small groups of two or three from others. The design is compact. The central section could house a disk unit for all four computers.

An alternative might be to designate specific computers for certain activities:

Computer #1 could be reserved for learning to program. In the event of heavy demand, time limits could be imposed on each user.

Computer #2 could be reserved for educational games, such as States and Capitals, Interactive Stories, Spanish, and so on.

Computer #3 could be used for playing Adventure games.

Computer #4 could be reserved for open activities, such as learning to write programs, word processing, financial calculations, and data base management.

There are as many possible designs for the physical space as there are rooms in your facility. Spend some time brainstorming ideas with people from the host site and your own staff on how best to configure your ComputerTown's physical environment.

Handling ComputerTown Equipment

Whenever groups of people work with equipment over an extended period of time, several common problems occur. The main causes for concern include equipment inventory, maintenance, repair, and replacement.

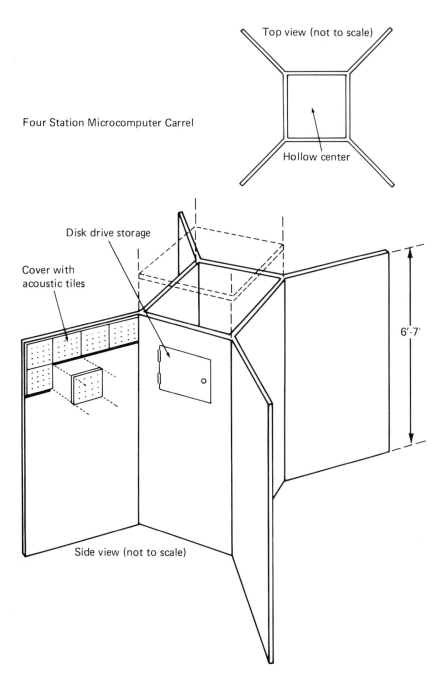

Top view (not to scale)

Four Station Microcomputer Carrel

Hollow center

Disk drive storage

Cover with
acoustic tiles

6'-7'

Side view (not to scale)

FIGURE 1. Four Station Microcomputer Carrel.

At ComputerTown, Menlo Park and ComputerTown, USA!
a variety of approaches to these problems were tried. At first,
ComputerTown, Menlo Park operated with borrowed computers
only. Each owner took charge of his or her machine and personal-
ly placed it in the hands of a friend when not attending the event.
Owners maintained their equipment and arranged for extra pe-
ripherals such as printers or large screens when needed. Owners
also provided whatever software they chose. Later, a box of cassette tapes with programs was placed near the computers for anyone to use. Occasionally, volunteers would inventory the box,
reorganize it, and replace damaged tapes.

After the first computers were donated to the Menlo Park Library, more formal plans had to be made. For the first year, while
the ComputerTown, USA! model was under development, Barbara Harvie, ComputerTown's library liaison, spent every afternoon at the library. Her duties included teaching, validating
library cards, checking out software tapes (which she kept organized and in working order), cleaning keyboards, and performing
other routine maintenance tasks. As library liaison, she also collected data on library use of computers and made observations of
ComputerTown visitor characteristics, such as sex, background,
level of experience upon first visit, speed of progress, and software preferences.

During the second year of the project, no staff person was
regularly assigned to the Menlo Park Library, and several computers were brought back to project headquarters a few blocks
away. A simple inventory and check-out system was instituted so
that anyone on staff could tell at a glance what equipment the
project had, where each individual piece of equipment was at that
moment, when it had last received maintenance, and its current
state of repair.

Please feel free to use the following model for your own inventory system.

Inventory

To set up the inventory system you need labels and a box of 5" ×
7" cards. Label each piece of hardware with a designated number.
It is important to number cartridges and switch boxes as well as

computers and monitors. A good rule of thumb is: if it can become separated, lost, or left behind, give it a number. Each numbered item should be represented by a card in your file box. At ComputerTown International, the cards look like this:

BRAND	**ITEM**	**NUMBER**

Serial Number: _____ Owner: _____

Date	Taken From	Taken To	By	Date Returned
3/1/81	Office	Jr. Museum	Liza	3/2/81
3/6/81	Office	CDC Repair	Ann	3/9/81

Notes on each item's state of repair can be added free form. Since a computer system is often composed of several inventory items, clip cards together to speed up the process of checking out whole systems. But resist the temptation to put several items on a single card, or you will have to make a whole new card each time you replace a connector cable. Handling separate cards also makes you less likely to forget small items when picking up or returning equipment.

Most of the time an inventory system may seem like an unnecessary hassle. However, it will pay off if anything ever does turn up missing. You will also find that the information collected by this system will help you decide on future equipment acquisition.

Equipment Maintenance

Computers, even little ones, are complex electronic gadgets. They will serve you well if given proper care, but they do have their frailties, and each will one day cross the threshold of being no longer worth repair.

It is a good idea to have a rotating maintenance schedule, taking one computer at a time to your local dealer for routine tune-up. This need not be too frequent if you can manage minor repairs yourself. There is nothing you can actually do at the keyboard to break a computer, although spontaneous internal problems could occur while you happen to be using one. If you suspect something is wrong with your machine, explore the following points before rushing it to the dealer for repair.

Preliminary Troubleshooting

1. Check all cords and connectors.
   - Is there power to each part of the system?
   - Are connectors plugged in all the way?
   - Are the wrong sockets connected together?
2. Check the monitor or TV.
   - Is it lit?
   - Is it turned on?
   - Is it plugged in?
   - Is the TV tuned to the correct channel?
   - Has someone been fiddling with the TV controls? (Check brightness, horizontal/vertical hold.)
   - Check the fuses.
3. Check tape recorders.
   - Try different tapes.
   - Check volume if applicable.
   - Clean tape heads (see below).
4. Check cartridge slots if you have them.
   - Are they dusty?
   - Is the cartridge firmly seated in its slot?
   - Are the edge connectors on the cartridge dirty? If so, wipe them clean and then polish them with a pencil eraser.
5. Check your computer's temperature. If it is hotter to the touch than usual, turn it off and let it cool. Many microcomputers will not function reliably in rooms warmer than 85° Farenheit. Even if the room seems cool to you, it is much hotter inside the machine.

Cleaning Tape Heads

The most common equipment problem encountered at Computer-Town, Menlo Park was caused by the cassette tape players on Commodore PETs and Radio Shack TRS-80s. Cleaning the tape heads regularly is good preventive maintenance.

The tape heads become coated with residues from the magnetic tape when the cassette players are heavily used. If the heads are not cleaned regularly, the tapes will not load correctly. The computer will respond with a LOAD ERROR message and the tape must be reloaded. To fix this, you will need:

- Cotton swabs
- Alcohol

Remove the cassette. Press the PLAY button and clean the protruding metal heads by rubbing them gently with a cotton swab dipped in alcohol. Try loading a tape again.

Cassette Control Button Malfunction

Cassette control buttons (FAST FORWARD, REWIND, and so on) can become loose in time. To rewind properly, you have to keep the REWIND button pressed down. If this problem occurs, take the recorder to the repair shop.

Troubleshooting Tapes

Sometimes it is not the tape player, but the tape itself which causes a problem. The tape surface wears out over time and should eventually be discarded. Watch out for fingerprints on the recording surface. The cure for fingerprints on the program section of the tape is to require that each person rewind the tape before removing it from the tape player. In this way, the user handles only the leader on the front of the tape.

Preventing Keyboard Problems

Keyboards can really take a beating in the public access environment. You can protect the top of each key by coating it with clear
fingernail polish.

Sticky Keys

Residue sometimes accumulates within the key mechanism and
prevents contact from taking place. Press each key several times.
If you have to apply undue pressure to make the letter appear on
the screen there is probably too much residue to allow the contact
to take place. Note how many times the key sticks or the letter
fails to appear on the screen.

The PETs at the Menlo Park Library needed keyboard cleaning once a month. The tools required for keyboard maintenance
are:

- Phillips screwdriver
- Tiny jeweler's screwdriver
- Cotton swabs
- Alcohol

Unplug the computer. Unscrew the hood of the PET with the
Phillips screwdriver and prop it up much like you would the hood
of a car. Using the jeweler's screwdriver, remove all the tiny
screws holding the contact board to the keyboard. Be careful not
to lose the screws. Lift the contact board away from the keyboard
while keeping the wires intact. Holding the contact board in one
hand, take a cotton swab dipped in alcohol and rub the contact
board. You can actually see the residue (fine, off-white powder).
If the board is particularly dirty, you may want to clean it again
with a new cotton swab. Clean the underside of the keyboard
which is still attached to the hood. Clean inside the round indenta-
tions. Replace the contact board with the tiny screws. This process
takes 15-20 minutes.

On computers with full-stroke keyboards, often the key tops
can be popped off with a knife or screwdriver, exposing the key

contact below. Check with your computer dealer or repair person to make sure you have this type of keyboard. If so, clean with cotton swabs and alcohol.

Fuse Trouble

Another source of machine malfunction and potential shock to the user involves the fuse.

On the PET, the fuse is located next to the toggle switch that turns on the machine. It is housed in a round plastic holder protruding from the back of the machine. Children often find this confusing because it resembles an "on/off" switch. As a result, the fuse often becomes loose, and needs to be placed in its holder and tightened. Be sure to unplug the machine before doing this!

With repeated misuse, the plastic casing surrounding the fuse may crack, making it difficult to seat the fuse properly. A temporary measure would be to secure the fuse cap with electrical tape until the machine can no longer function. By that time, you will want to take your machine down to your dealer for factory maintenance.

Other brands have fuses too, but they may not be easily accessible. Check your User's Guide or reference manual for details.

Of course, your building has fuses or circuit breakers also. If all the machines go off at once, check the building power. Another building power problem may be caused by other appliances (a refrigerator, for example) which generate electrical noise. This is passed along the power lines to each computer and may show up as distortion on each computer display. The cure for this is to buy a "line filter" for each computer or for the offending appliance. Plugged between the wall and the appliance, the filter may solve the problem.

Problems Beyond Your Scope

Every once in a while you may really have a sick computer which needs expert diagnosis and repair. If you can't get any response at all from your computer, if it fills its screen with gibberish, if it totally ignores the keyboard, gives you constant LOAD ERROR messages, or just stops running every few minutes, don't waste too much time trying to fix it yourself. Call your dealer and make arrangements for repair. Replacing one small chip or resoldering a wire may be all that is needed.

Hardware Security

There was no problem with stolen computers at the Menlo Park test site. If theft is a problem in your area, a locking pad can secure the computers to tables at a cost of about $70.00 each.

Several times, fuses were lost from the PET computers and machines were disabled. With a minor adjustment, the fuses were placed on the inside, making them inaccessible to the average user.

Software Storage: Selecting the Right Medium

Previous sections of this book have given advice on selecting and obtaining computers for your project. Not only will you have to choose what computers to add to your ComputerTown resources, but also what kind of storage medium to use: cassette, ROM cartridge, floppy diskette, or hard disk.

Cassettes can create complications at a public access ComputerTown. Cassette loading requires two to three minutes per tape. Also, since they fit so easily into a pocket, cassettes may tend to disappear. Cassettes are also fragile, especially when used by newcomers who do not know how to handle and care for them properly. These potential complications can be handled best by appointing one member of the project to make sure cassettes are being loaded and cared for properly by the users, and that they are in working order at all times.

The floppy diskette system is better for ComputerTown use because several games or other activities may be stored on one diskette, allowing visitors to review a catalog listing and select an activity. This takes less time than loading a cassette. Since the diskette contains several programs, maintenance, cataloging, and circulation are easier.

ROM cartridges have an extra convenience in that they are not as delicate as diskettes or tapes, and are every bit as easy to use. Of the three storage media, cartridges are the simplest to maintain and repair. Considering the amount of use your ComputerTown resources will receive, that's a strong point in favor of cartridges — if the computers you have or want to obtain can use cartridges. Not all computers are designed for cartridge software, though.

Hard disks can be added to many microcomputers, allowing you to store a large program library on this single medium. Hard disks are expensive compared to other storage media but they may pay off because of their speed, ease of use, and reliability.

Networking several small computers together so that they may share several floppy disk drives or a hard disk drive is also an excellent strategy. Many educational projects do this very successfully when there is a permanent facility for equipment.

Cataloging Software

A cataloging system will be necessary to avoid chaos, especially as your software collection grows in size and scope. The following system, used at ComputerTown, Menlo Park, was developed by teenage volunteer Niels Mortenson. It is user-oriented and deals only with cassette materials, since that was the only storage medium used at the Menlo Park site. The system provides the information one needs to know about the program when sitting down at the computer. Although it was designed for tapes used with the TRS-80, it can be easily modified for tapes used on other computers. Each tape is labeled as in Figure 2.

There are a number of codes available under "Tape Devices." They are:

(N) *No devices.* This means that no special devices are needed, and there are no special loading instructions.

(S) *Sound.* This means that the program has sound, so plug the AUX plug from the computer into a small amplifier to hear the sound.

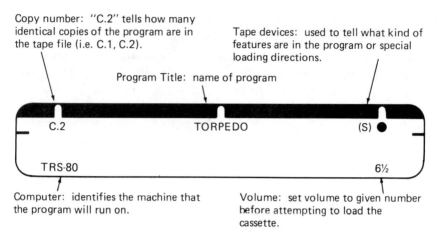

Copy number: "C.2" tells how many
identical copies of the program are in
the tape file (i.e. C.1, C.2).

Tape devices: used to tell what kind of
features are in the program or special
loading directions.

Program Title: name of program

Computer: identifies the machine that
the program will run on.

Volume: set volume to given number
before attempting to load the
cassette.

FIGURE 2. Tape Labeling Format.

(I) *Instructions.* This means that there is a sheet of directions for running or playing the program or game. Ask an aide for the instructions.

(•) *"System" dot.* The program is a "machine language" program and must be loaded under the "SYStem" comand.

All this information was coded on Dennison file folder labels, attached to both the cassette and its storage box. Using different colored labels allowed the computer tapes to be color coded by computer system. The codes were listed in a master catalog available to patrons. A sheet of instructions reminded patrons to rewind tapes, replace them in their storage boxes, and return them exactly where they were found.

While a cataloging system is helpful and necessary, don't be surprised when some chaos still occurs while using cassettes in a public access setting. Cassettes present a unique set of problems for cataloging and maintenance, especially when you are dealing with a variety of computers. Not only do you have different kinds, but variations within one category: two PETs may not be exactly alike, for example. Problems of this sort can be greatly eased by using diskettes or cartridges instead of cassettes. When disks or cartridges become disorganized with use, they can be sorted more easily.

Copyright Considerations

Software is copy-protected material. According to copyright laws, software should not be copied except for the personal use of the purchaser. This means that ComputerTown visitors should not take your software home to copy, nor should they make copies at ComputerTown. You can, however, make copies for your own use for backup and circulation within your own group.

Software Security

After losing several cassettes at the Menlo Park test site, the ComputerTown staff decided not to make the master tapes accessible to the public. The masters were needed to produce backup copies. The staff also discovered that the problem of disappearing tapes could be alleviated if the patrons were required to leave something of value, such as a driver's license, in exchange for the tape. Precautions of this sort are good practice, no matter what storage medium your ComputerTown uses.

Print Materials

Your most visible piece of ComputerTown courseware should be a simple, step-by-step set of materials on "How to Use This Computer," geared toward the absolute novice. After going through the validation process, visitors can turn to this booklet to begin their self-instruction. The "How to . . . " booklet and other fundamental print materials should be close to the computers for easy reference.

Books about computers and computing, especially those of interest to beginners, are also valuable reference materials. Since each microcomputer has its own BASIC language, it is important to have the right programming books for your particular machines. These books will be in high demand, especially when the machines are used to learn programming. One permanent reference copy of each volume could be kept near the appropriate computer, and two or three additional copies of each could be offered for circulation.

Resource lists are also very helpful in a self-teaching environment. Resources may be divided according to category of interest (classroom uses, business, hobbies, buying your own computer, and so forth). They can be further cataloged by format (newsletters, magazines, books, places, courses). Content descriptions need not be evaluative. You might consider offering printed copies of the most frequently used resource list for public dissemination.

B

Typical Questions at
ComputerTown Events

Many questions will come up as people explore computers for the first time. The following list contains questions the Computer-Town staff might have to answer at ComputerTown events.

Try to form a brief answer to each question as you read. If the answers come easily, you are well prepared. If you have a difficult time getting through the list, see that your project has access to someone who can assist you during question-and-answer sessions.

The following questions were asked at a ComputerTown event attended by over seventy visitors.

- What is ComputerTown?
- Do you have anything for sale?
- Which of the small color computers should I get for my kid as an educational toy?
- How many kinds of computers are there? How do I know which one to buy?
- What is 16K, 32K, 48K? How do I know which is best for me?
- When I read about computers in magazines and books, I don't understand the jargon. How can I learn the terminology?
- If I were entering the job market in this area, where would I go to get up to speed about computers?
- What career opportunities would be facilitated by my

knowing about computers? How do I go about exploring a career in the field?

- What are computer languages and how do they work? What is the difference between BASIC, Pascal, and the other languages I hear about? Which would be most useful to learn?

- What is the job of a program? How does it work? Would it be difficult for me to learn to program?

- Are there compilers for these machines?

- What is an operating system?

- Contrast the different machines' operating systems.

- Can I lease or rent a machine?

- What good is the machine beyond playing games?

- How does the Atari 800 compare to other machines? How does Brand X compare to Brand Y?

- Can I set up a machine so that it will search the Dow files and extract data on the stocks in my portfolio? How much will it cost? Will any machine let me tie into data bases like the Dow?

- How does a machine store data? Where does it store it?

- What is the difference between hardware and software?

- What are the cost tradeoffs in getting a computer? When do I know I can buy one effectively?

- When do I know that I need to move something onto the computer that I have been doing by hand?

- Why does a program take up space in the computer?

- Will the machines run Fortran, Cobol, and so on?

- Why should I buy one now? Why not wait for the newer machines?

- How can I justify spending XXX dollars for the computer, knowing that I will essentially throw it away in a few years?

- What will be the resale values of these things in a few years?

- What about assemblers/linkers for these small machines? What about software development tools?

- Can I put my software into a circuit (EPROM) so that it becomes part of the machine?
- Kids are beginning to use these things. What's going to happen to their education if they spend all their time on these devices?
- How do I know I am getting good software?
- Who sells software?
- If I read a magazine such as *Byte*, how can I tell from the advertisements what the software really does?
- Is there a beginner's magazine or book?
- Where are the users' groups in this area?
- If I have a complex problem in terms of putting hardware and software together, who can help me?
- Should I plan on doing my own programming, or can I get by without knowing how to program?
- What is a "turnkey" system?
- Will things become standardized in the future?
- How often do microcomputers break down?
- Can I get a broken machine fixed without difficulty?

How To Select a Personal Computer

Since many who attend your events will be interested in buying a computer of their own, your ComputerTown staff will often be asked for advice on choosing which one to buy. Feel free to help people but don't set yourself up as a free consultant under the ComputerTown banner, and remember that ComputerTown does not endorse any specific brand names.

In his article, "How to Select a Personal Computer" (*Recreational Computing*, July-August, 1981), David Thornburg offers invaluable suggestions to consumers in search of their dream machines:

"Hey! You know a lot about personal computers, which one should I buy?"

"If I had a nickel for each time I've heard that question, I'd be able to buy another computer myself," comments Thornburg. In answer to this ever-popular question, he has improvised a step-by-step procedure aimed at finding the perfect computer to suit an individual's specific needs:

1. Take out a big sheet of paper, labeled "Applications for My Dream Machine." List every single function you would like your ideal computer to serve. Will you use it for playing games, education, electronic mail, access to news wire services, personal finance, word processing, programming, mathematics, hobbies, home management? Whatever it is, list it here.

2. On your second sheet of paper, specify the features your computer will require for each application you have selected in list number one. Be sure to consider display, keyboard, joysticks, printers, phone connections, memory or floppy disk drives, etc.

3. Stumped? Don't panic! Take your list in hand and turn to:
   • Your local ComputerTown group
   • Computer fairs and expositions
   • Computer magazines
   • Manufacturer's catalogs
   • Users' groups
   • Computer stores

   It's no accident that the computer store ranks last on the list. A given store will only carry a limited line of computers. The wise consumer will begin the selection process with a broader base of information than can be gained from the dealers in retail stores.

4. Having selected your dream machine, the author suggests these final details: "Be sure the price quotation you receive includes everything you want—software and hardware. Ask about help in getting the system set up. Make sure the dealer is willing to support your purchase. Find out about warrantees, local service charges, and anything else that comes to mind."

Thornburg's article provides an excellent background for one of the most frequently asked questions at ComputerTown events. Use what he has outlined as a model to organize the information you will need to answer these frequent inquiries. You will no doubt expand upon this outline as you look about your community for resources and materials on the personal computer revolution.

C

Resources

Books

Introductory

Bork, Alfred. *Learning with Computers.* Bedford MA: Digital Press, 1981. A state-of-the-art assessment of basic philosophy and method for instructors using CAI technology.

Decken, Joseph. *The Electronic Cottage: Everyday Living with Your Personal Computer in the 1980's.* New York: William Morrow, 1981.

Evans, Christopher. *The Micro Millenium.* New York: Washington Square Press, 1979. Entertaining, mind-expanding, easily understood discussion of the development and future of computers.

Papert, Seymour. *Mindstorms.* New York: Basic Books, 1980. An excellent, important book by the designer of LOGO. Emphasis on how computers help children learn and not on how teachers teach. Focus on Piagetian discoveries, LOGO, and Turtle.

Peterson, Dale. *Big Things from Small Computers.* Reston VA: Reston Publishing Co., 1982. Delightful overview of how and where personal computers are being used — at work, home, and school.

Taylor, Robert (Ed.). *The Computer in the School: Tutor, Tool, Tutee.* New York: Teachers College Press, 1980. A collection of papers from seminal scholars in computers in education.

Computers in Education

Billings, Karen, & Morsund, David. *Are You Computer Literate?* Beaverton OR: Dilithium Press, 1979. Self-instruction format. Good introduction to capabilities, limitations, applications, and implications of computers.

Bork, Alfred (Ed.). *Computer Assisted Learning in Physics Education.* New York: Pergamon Press, 1980. A collection of papers that describe major projects from all over the world.

Burke, Robert. *CAI Sourcebook.* Englewood Cliffs NJ: Prentice-Hall, 1982. A step-by-step guide for CAI.

Doerr, Christine. *Microcomputers and the 3 R's.* Rochelle Park NJ: Hayden Book Co. A practical guide for teachers who want to get involved in computing. Has reliable suggestions on selecting a unit. Is also of value to users and administrators.

Dunlap, Mike, & Morsund, David. *Computers in Education Resource Handbook.* Eugene OR: University of Oregon, 1975. A good general resource. Areas covered are computers in education, teaching about computers, the computer as an aid to learning, the computer as a teacher and as a classroom management tool, and administrative uses of computers.

Edwards, J.B., Ellis, A.S., Richardson, D.E., Holznagel, D., & Klassen, D. *Computer Applications in Instruction: A Teacher's Guide to Selection and Use.* Hanover NH: Time Share Corp., 1978. A general introduction to uses of computers in education.

Harris, Diana (Ed.). *Proceedings of the National Educational Computing Conference.* Iowa City: University of Iowa, Weeg Computing Center, 1979. A collection of papers presented at the first NECC. All educational levels and disciplines are covered.

Kosel, Marge. *Elementary . . . My Dear Computer.* Lauderdale MN: Minnesota Educational Computing Consortium, 1978. This book has many lesson plans and programs for use in the elementary classroom using the computer.

Kurshan, Barbara. *Computer Literacy: Practical Ways to Teach the Basic Mathematical Skills.* Richmond VA: Virginia Council of Teachers of Mathematics, 1978. A curriculum guide for computer literacy. Includes goals and activities.

MicroSIFT: Evaluator's Guide for Microcomputer-Based Instructional Packages. Eugene OR: International Council for Computers in Education, 1982. Comprehensive plan for software evaluation—forms, samples, etc.

Morsund, David. *Calculators in the Classroom with Applications for Elementary and Middle School Teachers.* New York: Wiley, 1981. Basic text with good problems. Suitable for elementary pupils.

Morsund, David. *Introduction to Computers in Education for Elementary and Middle School Teachers.* Eugene OR: International Council for Computers in Education, 1981. Nonthreatening introduction for teachers. Contains 75 classroom activities for students.

Morsund, David. *Precollege Computer Literacy: A Personal Computing Approach.* Eugene OR: International Council for Computers in Education, 1982. Comprehensive definition of computer literacy.

Morsund, David. *School Administrator's Introduction to Instructional Use of Computers.* Eugene OR: International Council for Computers in Education, 1982. Discusses how computers are affecting educational content/process.

Naiman, Adeline. *Microcomputers in Education: An Introduction.* Chemsford MA: NEREX, 1982. New uses for computers in education and how to get started. Useful appendix of resources.

National Council of Teachers of Mathematics. *Guidelines for Evaluating Computerized Instructional Materials.* Reston VA: NCTM, 1981. Excellent software selection guide.

Nazzaro, Jean (Ed.). *Computer Connections for Gifted Children and Youth.* Reston VA: The Council for Exceptional Children, 1981. Basic information, resources, and projects for the gifted.

Peterson, Dale. *The Electronic Schoolhouse.* Reston VA: Reston Publishing Co., 1983.

Poirot, James. *Computers and Education.* Manchaca TX: Sterling Swift, 1980. An interesting introductory book.

Ricketts, Dick. *Course Goals in Computer Education K-12.* Portland OR: Commercial Educational Distributing Service, 1979. Covers computer literacy, data processing, programming, etc.

Rogers, Jean. *An Introduction to Computers and Computing.* Eugene OR: International Council for Computers in Education, 1981. Complete outline for a high school course in computer science.

What Is a Computer?

Ball, Marion. *What Is a Computer?* Boston MA: Houghton Mifflin, 1972. Covers the areas of what is a computer, history, parts of the system, how software is made. Includes a summary, glossary, and index.

Ball, Marion J., & Charp, Sylvia. *Be a Computer Literate.* Morristown NJ: Creative Computing Press. An introduction to the computer world for children. Full color diagrams, drawings, and large type make this book easy to read and use.

Berger, Melvin. *Those Amazing Computers!* "Science is What and Why Series." New York: Day, 1973. Illustrated with photographs and organized by uses. Includes bibliography, brief material on input, output, control unit, programming, flow charts, memory, and data banks.

DeRossi, Claude. *Computers: Tools for Today.* Chicago IL: Children's Press, 1972. Gives simple information about binary addition, bits, punched cards, card readers, magnetic tape, programming, programmers, flow charts, and a little history.

D'Idgnazio, Fred. *Katie and the Computer.* Morristown NJ: Creative Computing Press, 1978. A picture book adventure that explains how a computer works to a child. It is both an exciting story that a child will want to read and a simple explanation of computers.

Kenyon, Raymond G. *I Can Learn About Calculators and Computers.* New York: Harper & Row, 1961. A "how to build your own" and includes history and "how to" about computers.

Meadow, Charles. *The Story of Computers.* New York: Harvey House, 1970. Simple and clear information on computers. A glossary, index, bibliography, and table of contents are included.

Rusch, Richard B. *Computers: Their History and How They*

Work. New York: Simon & Schuster, 1969. Gives a clear idea of the computer's role, its physical equipment, and current and future applications. It is not a primer and does not go into detail on programming.

Rice, Jean. *My Friend — The Computer.* Minneapolis MN: T.S. Dension, 1976. A very simplified explanation of the computer, its uses, development, operation, input procedures, flow charts, programming, and terms.

Srivastava, Jane Jonas. *Computers.* New York: Thomas Y. Crowell Co., 1972. This short book, in the "Young Math Book" Series, explains the computer as a counting machine. Other topics include programmers, languages, input, printouts, control units, flow charts, uses of computers, and history. The information is presented very simply.

Wall, Elizabeth S. *Computer Alphabet Book.* Nokomis FL: Bayshore Books, 1979. The first of a series of a "Beginning Computer Literacy" series. It is an introduction to computers with alphabetized, simple definitions and explanations of computer parts, terms, etc.

Willis, Jerry. *The Peanut Butter and Jelly Guide to Computers.* Mountain View CA: Creative Publications, 1980. A simple introduction to computers. It explains what a computer can do and how it does it.

Programming and Using the Computer

Abelson, Harold, & DiSessa, A. *Turtle Geometry.* 1981. A detailed innovative use of the computer (LOGO, etc.) to teach geometric concepts at the high school and college levels.

Ahl, David H. *BASIC Computer Games.* Morristown NJ: Creative Computing. This book contains a variety of computer games with descriptions of each and computer limitations.

Ahl, David H. *Getting Started in Classroom Computing.* Maynard MA: Digital Equipment Corp., 1974. The games in this booklet introduce the newcomer to using games and computers in the classroom.

Albrecht, Bob et al. *ATARI BASIC.* New York: Wiley, 1980.

Albrecht, Bob et al. *BASIC* (2nd ed.). New York: Wiley, 1980.

Albrecht, Bob et al. *BASIC for Home Computers.* New York: Wiley, 1981.

Albrecht, Bob et al. *TRS-80 BASIC.* New York: Wiley, 1981.

Albrecht, Bob. *TRS-80 Color Computer.* New York: Wiley, 1982.

Brainerd, Walter and Others. *Introduction to Computer Programming.* New York: Harper, 1979. Introduction to what computers can do. Concepts can be transferred to specific computer languages.

Braude, Michael. *Larry Learns About Computers.* Minneapolis MN: T.S. Denison Co., 1969. Explains, in a simple manner, about the history, uses, and terms in computers.

Conlon, Jim, & Deliman, T. *ATARI PILOT for Beginners.* Reston VA: Reston Publishing Co., 1982.

Dwyer, Thomas A., & Kaufman, Michael S. *A Guided Tour of Computer Programming in BASIC.* Boston MA: Houghton Mifflin, 1980. This book is on communicating in the BASIC language and showing the student how to use the computer. BASIC vocabulary is introduced and key words and explanations of input and other commands are given. There is also a section on two-dimensional arrays, "library" functions.

Dwyer, Thomas A., & Critchfield, Margot. *BASIC and the Personal Computer.* Reading MA: Addison-Wesley, 1979. An excellent book with which to learn BASIC. Covers graphics in addition to elementary commands. Many sample programs are included.

Ellis, Allan B. *The Use and Misuse of Computers in Education.* New York: McGraw-Hill, 1974. This book points out that sometimes computers are misused in schools. The computer is defined in the book and some uses are given. A computer system for guidance is given as an example of a project.

Engel, C.W. *Stimulating Simulations.* Mountain View CA: Creative Publications. The book is a series of real world simulations. For each of the 12 simulations, a listing, flow chart, and sample runs are included.

Graham, Neill. *The Mind Tool: Computers and Their Impact on Society* (2nd ed.). St. Paul MN: West Publishing Co., 1980. A review of computers with short and informative chapters on computer applications in many different areas, as well as an introduction to BASIC.

Haskell, Michael. *A First Course in Computing.* New York: McGraw-Hill, 1982. An excellent introductory course.

Horn, Carin, & Poirot, J. *Computer Literacy: Problem Solving with Computers.* Manchaca TX: Sterling Swift, 1981. A suitable secondary school computer literacy text. Some BASIC programming.

Inman, Don, & Inman, Kurt. *Apple Machine Language.* Reston VA: Reston Publishing Co., 1980. Machine language programming on the Apple in small, easy steps. Requires knowledge of BASIC.

Inman, Don, & Inman, Kurt. *The ATARI Assembler.* Reston VA: Reston Publishing Co., 1982. Simple detailed directions for using the ATARI Assembler with the ATARI 400 or 800 model computer.

Inman, Don et al., *Introduction to TI BASIC.* Rochelle Park NJ: Hayden, 1980.

Inman, Don et al. *More TRS-80 BASIC.* New York: Wiley, 1981.

Inman, Don, & Dymax. *TRS-80 Color Computer Graphics.* Reston VA: Reston Publishing Co., 1982. Helps the user discover the ability to create interesting color computer graphics that can enhance programs.

Inman, Don et al. *TRS-80 Pocket Computer.* New York: Wiley, 1982.

Johnson, M. Clemens. *Educational Uses of the Computer: An Introduction.* Chicago IL: Rand McNally, 1970. This book is a concise and nontechnical introduction to the variety of uses of the computer in education. It contains chapters on student data, computer assistance in instruction and in research, classroom problem solving, assisting the teacher in classroom management, and research skills in education.

Kohl, Herb, Kahn, Ted, & Lindsay, Len. *ATARI Games and Recreation.* Reston VA: Reston Publishing Co., 1981. A unique book that teaches a beginner the skills of computer programming through games.

Kohn, Bernice. *Computers at Your Service.* Englewood Cliffs NJ: Prentice-Hall, 1962. Seventy-two pages with illustrations on the computer by Aliki.

Luehrmann, Arthur, & Peckham, H. *Apple PASCAL: A Hands-On Approach.* New York: McGraw-Hill, 1981. Introductory manual on PASCAL and Apple computers. Includes problems with solutions.

Lewis, William. *Problem Solving Principles for Programmers: Applied Logic, Psychology, and Grit.* Rochelle Park NJ: Hayden, 1980. Lyrical treatment that uses brain teasers, short problems, algorithmic design, structured programming, and debugging.

McQuigg, James D., & Harness, Alto M. *Flowcharting.* Boston MA: Houghton Mifflin, 1970. A workbook on flowcharting.

Morsund, David. *BASIC Programming for Computer Literacy.* New York: McGraw-Hill, 1978. A text module for the computer programming of computer literacy instruction. It teaches BASIC.

Pattis, Richard. *Karel, the Robot: A Gentle Introduction to the Art of Programming.* New York: Wiley, 1981. From physical to abstract representations — gently. Simple four-session introduction.

Rogowski, Stephen J. *Computer Clippings.* Mountain View CA: Creative Publications. The book includes 50 problems with a sample solution for each. Graphics are included.

Spencer, Donald D. *Using BASIC in the Classroom.* Ormond Beach FL: Camelot Publishing Co. Aimed at the beginning teacher of the BASIC computer language.

Stern, Nancy. *Flowcharting — A Self-Teaching Guide.* New York: Wiley, 1975. A clear introduction to the use of flowcharting.

Wadsworth, Nat. *Introduction to Low Resolution Graphics.* Mountain View CA: Creative Publications. The book introduces graphics that can be applied on the Apple, PET, or TRS-80. Projects include simple shape programs through animation.

Waite, Michael. *Computer Graphics Primer.* Mountain View CA: Creative Publications. The book introduces graphics. It includes plotting lines, curves, and special characters. It is written for Apple high-resolution graphics.

Zamora, Ramon, Scarvie, William, & Albrecht, Bob. *PET*

BASIC I. Reston VA: Reston Publishing Co., 1981. Creative use of graphics, open page formats, humor, and interesting small programs to type and try.

Zamora, Ramon et al. *Teach Yourself TI LOGO.* Peterborough NH: Byte, 1983

Zamora, Ramon, Inman, Don, & Albrecht, Bob. *VIC BASIC.* Reston VA: Reston Publishing Co., 1983.

Fiction

Christopher, John. *The White Mountains.* New York: Mac-Millan, 1967.

Del Rey, Lester. *The Runaway Robot.* Philadelphia PA: Westminster, 1965.

Fairman, Paul W. *The Forgetful Robot.* New York: Holt Rinehart and Winston, 1968.

Hayes, William. *Hold That Computer!* New York: Atheneum, 1968.

Norton, Andre. *The Beast Master.* New York, Harcourt Brace, 1965.

Philbrook, Clem. *Ollie's Team and the Football Computer.* Philadelphia PA: Hastings, 1968.

Steadman, Ralph. *Little Red Computer.* New York: McGraw-Hill, 1969.

Van Tassel, Dennie L. (Ed.). *Computers, Computers! in Fiction and in Verse.* New York: Thomas Nelson Inc., 1977. This is a collection of eleven short stories, fiction, nonfiction, and verse on computers.

Miscellaneous

Davis, William, & McCormack A. *The Information Age.* Reading MA: Addison-Wesley, 1979. An overview of the impact of computers, basic technology, uses, problems, and future.

Fishman, Katherine D. *The Computer Establishment.* New York: Harper & Row, 1981. An inside look into the growth and direction of the computer industry.

Graham, Neil. *The Mind Tool.* St. Paul MN: West Publishing
Co., 1980. Comprehensive book suitable for high school computer literacy classes.

Kent, Ernest. *The Brains of Men and Machines.* Peterborough
NH: Byte-McGraw-Hill, 1981. Compares mechanics of human
and machine intelligence, memory, etc.

Leavitt, Ruth. *Artist and Computer.* New York: Harmony Books,
1976. Computer art, artists.

McCorduck, Pamela. *Machines Who Think.* San Francisco CA:
Freeman, 1979. History of AI.

Mowshowitz, Abbe. *Inside Information: Computers in Fiction.*
Reading MA: Addison-Wesley, 1977. Collection that presents a
unique view of the computer through novelists' eyes.

Parker, Donn. *Crime by Computer.* New York: Scribner's, 1976.
A fascinating look at a growing problem by the leading expert
on the history of computer crime.

Raphael, Bertram. *The Thinking Computer.* San Francisco CA:
Freeman, 1976. Past, present, and future of AI.

Silver, Gerald. *The Social Impact of Computers.* New York: Harcourt, 1979.

Smith, Robert Ellis. *Privacy: How to Protect What's Left of It.*
Garden City NY: Anchor Press, 1979. Overview of issues con-
cerning privacy and computerization.

Waite, Mitchell. *Computer Graphics Primer.* Indianapolis IN:
Howard Sams Co., 1979. Instruction on production of video
graphics in Apple BASIC. Easily adaptable to PET and TRS-
80.

Weizenbaum, Joseph. *Computer Power and Human Reason.* San
Francsico CA: Freeman, 1976. Excellent introduction to the
ethical/social issues of widespread computer usage.

Winston, Patrick Henry. *Artificial Intelligence.* Reading MA:
Addison-Wesley, 1977. Survey of AI with emphasis on LISP.

Films

Bibliography: Lidtke, Doris. *Computer and Computer Applica-*

tions: A Film Bibliography. Portland OR: Oregon Council for Computer Education, 1977.

A Day in the Life of a Computer, J. Weston Walsh, Publisher, Portland, Maine 04104.

Art from Computers, 8 minutes, Control Data Corporation.

At Home 2001, 24 minutes, New Hyde Park, New York, Modern Talking Pictures.

Careers in Computers, Pathescope, Educational Films.

The Catalyst, 13 minutes, Sperry Univac, Blue Bell, Pennsylvania.

Clinical Uses of the Computer, Control Data Corporation, Minneapolis, Minnesota.

The Computer, 11 minutes, Control Data Corporation, Minneapolis, Minnesota.

Computer Revolution Part 1, New Hyde Park, New York, Modern Talking Pictures.

Computer Revolution Part 2, New Hyde Park, New York, Modern Talking Pictures.

IBM: Close Up, 21 minutes, New Hyde Park, New York, Modern Talking Pictures.

IBM World's Fair Puppet Show, 10 minutes, New Hyde Park, New York, Modern Talking Pictures.

The Information Machine, 11 minutes, Modern Talking Pictures.

Introduction to Digital Computers, 24 minutes, Sperry Univac.

The Endless Revolution, Sperry Univac.

Thinking?? Machine, 19 minutes, BELL Telephone.

2001, 25 minutes, Rarigs, Seattle, Washington.

Year 1999 A.D., Ford Motor Company, B.U. Film Library.

Magazines

AEDS Journal. Association of Educational Data Systems, 1201 Sixteenth Street, N.W., Washington DC 20036.

Antic, 297 Missouri Street, San Francisco CA 94107

Byte Magazine, 70 Main Street, Peterborough NH 03458.

Compute! Small System Services, Inc., P.O. Box 5406, Greensboro NC 27403.

Computers and Education. Pergamon Press, Inc., Maxwell House, Fairview Park, Elmsford NY 10523.

The Computing Teacher. Computing Center, Eastern Oregon State College, LaGrande OR 97850.

Creative Computing. Creative Computing, P.O. Box 789-M, Morristown NJ 07960.

Creative Computing. Creative Computing Catalog, 39 East Hanover Street, Morris Plains NJ 07950.

Courseware Magazine, 4919 Millbrook, Suite 222A, Fresno CA 93426.

edu. The Education Products Group Magazine of Digital Equipment Corporation, Educ Products Group, DEC, Maynard MA 01754.

Educational Computing. MAGSUB, Ltd., Oakfield House, Perrymount Road, Haywards Heath, Sussex RH16 3DH, England.

Educom, P.O. Box 364, Princeton NJ 08540.

Electronic Games. Reese Publishing Company, Inc., 235 Park Avenue South, New York NY 10003.

Electronic Learning, 902 Sylvan Avenue, Englewood Cliffs NJ 07632.

Games, P.O. Box 10145, Des Moines IA 50340.

InfoWorld, 530 Lytton Avenue, Palo Alto CA 94301.

Interface Age Magazine. McPheters, Wolfe, & Jones, 16704 Marquardt Avenue, Cerritos CA 90701.

Journal of Educational Data Processing. IDEOS, P.O. Box 867, Soquel CA 95073.

Kilobaud Microcomputing. Wayne Green, Inc., 80 Pine Street, Peterborough NH 03458.

Learning Magazine, 530 University Avenue, Palo Alto CA 94301.

Microcomputer Index. Microcomputer Information Services, 3070 Adams Way, Santa Clara CA 95051.

Personal Computing, 4 Disk Drive, Box 1408, Riverton NJ 08077.

Popular Computing. Byte Publications, Inc., 70 Main Street, Peterborough NH 03458.

Scholastic Inc. Educational Software, 904 Sylvan Avenue, Englewood Cliffs NJ 07632.

SIGUE Bulletin. Computer Uses in Education, Association for Computing Machinery, 1133 Avenue of the Americas, New York NY 10036.

T.H.E. Journal. Information Synergy, Inc. P.O. Box 992, Acton MA 01720.

80 Microcomputing. 1001001, Inc., 80 Pine Street, Peterborough NH 03458.

80 Microcomputing, P.O. Box 306, Dalton CA 01226.

'99er. Emerald Valley Publishing Company, P.O. Box 5537, Eugene OR 97405.

Organizations

American Federation of Information Processing Societies, 210 Summit Avenue, Montvale NJ 07645.

Association for Computing Machinery, 211 East 43rd Street, New York NY 10017.

Association for Educational Data Systems, 12021 Sixteenth Street, N.W., Washington DC 20036.

CUE (Computer-Using Educators), P.O. Box 18547, San Jose CA 95158.

International Council for Computers in Education (ICCE), Department of Computer and Information Science, University of Oregon, Eugene OR 97403.

Minnesota Educational Computing Consortium (MECC), 2520 Broadway Drive, Lauderdale MN 55113.

National Council of Teachers of Mathematics, 1906 Association Drive, Reston VA 22091.

Oregon Council for Computer Education, 4015 S.W. Canyon Road, Portland OR 97221.

D

ComputerTown
Affiliate Sites

USA

Alaska

Tri Valley Community Library
Box 60
Healy AK 99743

Arizona

Royal Palm Jr. High
Attn: Fred Cheshire
8520 North 19th Avenue
Phoenix AZ 85021

California

Center for Math Literacy
Attn: Jose Gutierrez
San Francisco State University
1600 Holloway Avenue
San Francisco CA 94132

Corte Madera School
4575 Alpine Road
Portola Valley CA 94025

Cragmont School
Attn: Lynn Alper/Nancy Charl-
son
830 Regal Road
Berkeley CA 94708

Glendora Public Library
Attn: Laura Winningham
140 South Glendora Avenue
Glendora CA 91740

Encinal Summer Session
Encinal School
Atherton CA 94025

Hoover Boys' Club
Attn: Margo Ritter
400 Market Place
Menlo Park CA 94025

Inst. for Educational Improvement
231 E. Millbrae Avenue
Millbrae CA 94035

Kittredge School
2355 Lake Street
San Francisco CA 94121

Lawrence Hall of Science
Science & Math Education Library
Centennial Drive
Berkeley CA 94720

Menlo-Atherton High School
Attn: Peggy Charleton
Ringwood & Middlefield
Atherton CA 94025

Menlo Park Public Library
Attn: Doreen Cohen
Alma & Ravenswood
Menlo Park CA 94025

National University
School of Education
174 Camino Corto
Vista CA 92083

Old Mill School
Mill Valley CA 94941

Palo Alto Junior Museum
1451 Middlefield Road
Palo Alto CA 94303

Petaluma High School
201 Fair Street
Petaluma CA 94952

Richard School
910 East Borden Road
San Marios CA 92069

San Bernadino Public Library
Attn: Mike Clark
401 North Arrowhead Avenue
San Bernadino CA 92401

San Mateo County Office of Educ.

333 Main Street
Redwood City CA 94063

Sausalito Public Library
420 Litho Street
Sausalito CA 94965

Sonoma City Library
Third & E Streets
Santa Rosa CA 95404

Colorado

Aspen Computer Society
Attn: Richard Sherman
Box 5110
Aspen CO 81612

Aurora Public Library
14949 East Alameda Drive
Aurora CO 80012

Pike's Peak Library District
Attn: Anne E. Harrington
P.O. Box 1579
Colorado Springs CO 80901

Connecticut

Shepaug Valley School
South Street
Washington CT 06793

Weston Public Schools
135 School Road
Weston CT 06883

Wilton Public Schools
Box 277
Wilton CT 06897

Florida

ComputerTown New Smyrna
  Beach
Attn: Klem Majeckie
Brannon Memorial Library
105 South Riverside Drive
New Smyrna Beach FL 32069

Lincoln Community High School
Attn: Larry Nelson
1000 Primm Road
Lincoln FL 62656

Oak Hill Elementary
Attn: Champee Kemp
Chinquapin Drive
Eglin AFB FL 32542

Rand Junior High School
2500 North Arlington Hts. Road
Arlington Heights FL 60004

Venice Area Public Library
300 South Nokomis Avenue
Venice FL 33595

Walton Middle School
Attn: Gayle Wilkerson
Georgia Street
Defuniak Springs FL 32433

Georgia

Paide 1A School
Attn: Kathy Stone
1509 Ponce De Leon Avenue
Atlanta GA 30307

West Georgia College
Attn: Jerry Trammell, Jr.
Continuing Education

Adamson Hall
Carrollton GA 30113

Idaho

Idaho State University
Box 8322
Pocatello ID 83209

Iowa

Harlan Community Library
718 Court Street
Harlan IA 51537

Illinois

Chicago Public Library
Attn: Emelie Shroder
Technical Division
425 North Michigan
Chicago IL 60611

Chicago Public Library
North Pulaski Branch
4041 West North Avenue
Chicago IL 60639

Chicago Public Library
West Belmont Branch
3204 North Narragansett Avenue
Chicago IL 60634

ComputerTown Barrington
Attn: Holly Anderson
Route 2, Barrington Bourne
Barrington Hills IL 60010

Dakota C.O. 201
Dakota IL 61018

David Shimberg
6856 North Glenwood
Chicago IL 60626

Eureka High School
District Unit No. 140
200 West Cruger
Eureka IL 61530

Glenview Public Library
1930 Glenview Road
Glenview IL 60025

Kishwaukee College
Malta IL 60150

Rhodes School
Attn: Judy Henry
8931 West Fullerton
River Grove IL 60171

Southern Illinois University
Attn: Dr. Charles Turner
Box 122
Edwardsville IL 62026

Stanford Grade School
Grant Street
Stanford IL 61774

Weed Dale Jr. High School
Attn: Marilyn Probst
6N655 Wood Dale Road
Wood Dale IL 60191

Indiana

Carroll High School
3701 Carroll Road
Fort Wayne IN 46818

Erlham College
Richmond IN 47374

Indiana University at South Bend
1700 Mishawaka Avenue
P.O. Box 7111
South Bend IN 46615

Solon Robinson Elem. School
Wells & Pettibone
Crown Point IN 46307

Taylor University
Attn: R. Waldo Roth
Upland IN 46989

Warsaw Community Schools
Atwood School
Box 128
Atwood IN 46502

Kansas

Goodland High School Library
1209 Cherry
Goodland KS 67735

Topeka Public Schools
Attn: Paul Mitschler
624 West 24th Street
Topeka KS 66611

Kentucky

Jefferson County Public Schools
Attn: Claudia M. Reeves
Educational Media Center
4409 Preston Highway
Louisville KY 40213

Kentucky Cooperative Ext. Service
Room S-327, Ag. Sci.
North University of Kentucky
Lexington KY 40546

University of Louisville
Attn: Janet Morris
School of Education
Louisville KY 40292

Maryland

Montgomery Cnty. Dept. of
  Public Libraries
99 Maryland Avenue
Rockville MD 20850

Montgomery Cnty. Public
  Schools
Attn: Marlin Heckendorn
850 Hungerford Drive
Rockville MD 20850

North Chevy Chase Center for
  Specialized and Interrelated Instruction
3700 Jones Bridge Road
Chevy Chase MD 20815

Massachusetts

Boston College
140 Commonwealth Avenue
Chestnut Hill MA 02167

Michigan

Grace A. Dow Memorial Library
1710 West St. Andrews
Midland MI 48640

Impression 5 Museum
200 Museum Drive
Lansing MI 48933

Linderman School
124 3rd Avenue East

Kalispell MI 49901

Michigan Technological Univer-
  sity
Attn: James Spain
Houghton MI 49431

Miller Elementary School
850 Spencer Road
Brighton MI 48116

Northport Public Schools
Attn: Grace Snyder
104 Wing
Northport MI 49610

REMC-9 Saginaw I.S.D.
6235 Gratiot Road
Saginaw MI 48602

Stevensville Public Schools
District No. 2
300 Park Street
Stevensville MI 59870

Willard Library
7 West Van Buren
Battle Creek MI 49017

Minnesota

Baldwin Public Library
990 Maple
St. Paul MN 55106

East Central Regional Library
2445 Birch
Cambridge MN 55008

Mankato State University
Memorial Library
19 MSU
Mankato MN 56001

Missouri

Hayti School
400 North Fourth Street
Hayti MO 63851

Washington University
Attn: Pat Taylor
Lindell & Skinker Campus Box
St. Louis MO 63130

Montana

Butte High School
401 S. Wyoming
Butte MT 59701

Nebraska

Nebraska Business Dev. Center
Attn: Sharise Backer
Wayne State College
Wayne NE 68771

New Jersey

Brookside School
Brookside Avenue
Allendale NJ 07452

Franklin Township Schools
Attn: John J. Hopton
Macapee Road
Somerset NJ 08873

New Jersey Inst. of Technology
323 High Street
Newark NJ 07102

Ridgewood Board of Education

Attn: Gail Finlay
155 Washington Place
Ridgewood NJ 07450

South Main Street School
701 South Main Street
Pleasantville NJ 08232

New York

Adriance Memorial Library
93 Market Street
Poughkeepsie NY 12601

Altamont Elementary School
Attn: J. York
Altamont NY 12009

Department of Technology and
   Society
SUNY at Stony Brook
Stony Brook NY 11794

Fairport Public Library
1 Village Landing
Fairport NY 14450

Glen Cove Schools
Attn: Herb Mummers
Doris Lane
Glen Cove NY 11542

Haverstraw Stony Point Central
   School District
117 Main Street
Stony Point NY 10980

Hobart and William Smith Col-
   leges
Attn: Jack D. Harris
Department of Sociology
Geneva NY 14456

Huntington Public Library
338 Main Street
Huntington NY 11743

Imagination Project
65 Middaugh Road
Brooktondal NY 14817

John C. Hart Memorial Library
1130 Main Street
Shrub Oak NY 10588

Kent Free Public Library
42 Smadbeck Avenue
Carmel NY 10512

Liverpool Public Library
2nd & Tulip Streets
Liverpool NY 13088

Massapequa Public Schools
Attn: Diane Yaris
4925 Merrick Road
Massapequa NY 11758

Roosevelt Public Library
Rose & Mansfield Avenues
Roosevelt NY 11575

Sherman Central School
Park Street
Sherman NY 14781

Sherrill Elementary
Attn: Tom Kescikeniak
217 Kinsley Street
Sherrill NY 13461

Wilson Central School District
Attn: Steven J. La Rock
412 Lake Street
Wilson NY 14172

North Carolina

Northeast Regional Education Center
P.O. Box 1028
Williamston NC 27892

North Dakota

Standing Rock Community College
Fort Yates
Fort Yates ND 58538

Ohio

CP & You Computer Learning Center
Attn: Dr. Howard Moskowitz
5903 Elmer Drive
Toledo OH 43615

Fairfield County District Library
219 North Broad Street
Lancaster OH 43130

Oklahoma

ComputerTown, OK!
Attn: D. Skvaria/E. Minor/C. Hall
Pioneer Multi-County Library
225 North Webster
Norman OK 73069

Oklahoma State Dept. of Educ.
Attn: Susan Wheeler
Instr. Computer Resource Center
2500 North Lincoln
Oklahoma City OK 73105

Oregon

Professional Library
Roseburg Public Schools
948 S.E. Roberts
Roseburg OR 97470

Salem Public Library
585 Liberty Street, S.E.
Salem Oregon 97301

Pennsylvania

Abraham Lincoln Jr. High School
Attn: M. Finkelstein/J. Holl-
   inger
1001 Lehigh Avenue
Lancaster PA 17602

Huntingdon Valley Library
654 Red Lion Road
Huntingdon Valley PA 19006

Nether – Providence   Middle
   School
200 S. Providence Road
Wallingford PA 19086

Northland Public Library
300 Cumberland Road
Pittsburgh PA 15237

Titusville Area Schools
302 East Walnut
Titusville PA 16554

South Carolina

No. 1 Teacher Center
Attn: Jim Hockman

Richland County School Dist.
   One
2600 Barhamville Road
Columbia SC 29204

Tennessee

Microcomputer Access for the
   Visually Impaired Project
Box 328, Peabody of Vanderbilt
Nashville TN 37203

Texas

Austin Public Library
Attn: Kent Middleton
Information Services
P.O. Box 2282
Austin, TX 78768

Region III Education Service
   Cent.
1905 Leary Lane
Victoria TX 77901

Vanguard School
2517 Mount Carmel
Waco TX 76710

Virginia

Educational Media Center
Alexandria City Public Schools
3801 West Braddock Road
Alexandria VA 22302

Hollins College
4940 Buckhorn Road
Roanoke VA 24020

Washington

Community Resource Center
Attn: Marlene Curtis/Ron Baker
Wenatchee Valley College
Wenatchee WA 98801

Washington, D.C.

Capital Children's Museum
Attn: Ann White Lewin
800 3rd Street, N.E.
Washington, D.C. 20002

Wisconsin

Bullen Junior High School Library
2804 39th Avenue
Kenosha WI 53142

Hillcrest Elementary School Library
1200 Milea Street
Eau Claire WI 54701

Hinds Junior College
Attn: Tony Woods
1750 Chadwick Drive
Jackson WI 39204

John Bennin, Project Director
620 Hill Street
West Baraboo WI 53913

Marshfield Sr. High School
1401 East Becker Road
Marshfield WI 54449

Mineral Point Unified Schools

Attn: William F. Dagnon
706 Ridge Street
Mineral Point, WI 53565

Rice Lake High School Library
30 South Wisconsin Avenue
Rice Lake WI 54868

School of Library and Information Science
University of Wisc. — Milwaukee
P.O. Box 413
Milwaukee WI 53201

University of Wisconsin — River Falls
River Falls WI 54022

Women's Studies Librarian at Large
112A Memorial
728 State
Madison WI 53706

BANGLADESH

American International School
Dacca, Bangladesh
c/o Department of State
Washington DC 20520

CANADA

Etobicoke Public Library
P.O. Box 501
Etobicoke, Ontario M9C 5G1

Hamilton Public Library
Kenilworth Branch
103 Kenilworth Avenue North
Hamilton, Ontario L8H 4R6

GERMANY

Winifried Hofacker
Ing. W. Hofacker GMBH
8 Munchen 75
Postfach 437

POLAND

From U.S.A.

The American School of Warsaw
c/o American Consulate General
Attn: Larry Strong
Siessmeirstrasse 19/21
Frankfurt Am Main, W. Germany

From Europe

The American School of Warsaw
Attn: Larry Strong
c/o American Embassy (WAW)
APO New York NY 09757

UNITED KINGDOM

David Tebbutt, Project Director
7 Collins Dr., Eastcote
Middlesex HA4 9EL

ComputerTown Croydon
(Vernon Gifford)
111 Selhurst Road, Croydon
London SE25 6LH

CTUK Ealing (Mike Baker)
5 Edinburgh Road, Hanwell
London W4 3JY

CT Enfield (Alan S. Waring)
50 Drayton Gardens
Winchmore Hill
London N21 2NS

CTUK Caversham Park Village
(Patrick Colley)
52 Queensway
Caversham Park Village
Reading, Berks RG4 0SJ

ComputerTown Wokingham
(Alan Sutcliffe)
4 Binfield Road, Wokingham
Berkshire RG11 1SL

CTNE Gateshead
(John Stephen Bone)
2 Claremont Place, Gateshead
Tyne & Wear NE8 1TL

CTNE South Shields
(Richard Powell)
22 Downham Court
South Shields
Tyne & Wear

CTNE Newcastle upon Tyne
(Steven Christian)
51 Burnstones, West Denton
Newcastle upon Tyne NE5 2DF

Colchester Computer Society
(Pete Shaw)
15 St. Vincent Road
Clacton on Sea
Essex CO15 1NA

CTUK Romford (Phillip Joy)
130 Rush Green Road
Romford, Essex

ComputerTown Eastcote
(David Tebbutt)
7 Collins Drive, Eastcote
Middlesex HA4 9EL

ComputerTown Glouchester
(Steve Haynes)
5 Guinea Street, Kingholm
Gloucester GL1 3BL

Horsham ComputerTown
(Andrew Holyer)
10 Masons Field, Mannings Heath
Horsham, Sussex RH13 6JP

ComputerTown Street
(Tom Graves)
19a West End Street
Somerset BA16 0LQ

ComputerTown Retford

(Bill Gibbins)
3 Longholme Road, Retford
Notts ND22 6TU

ComputerTown, New Addington
(Brigett Gorton)
18 Purbright Crescent
New Addington
Croydon CR0 0RT

ComputerTown Renold Ltd.
(Keith Taylor)
Carter Hydraulic Works
Thornbury
Bradford BD3 8HG

CTUK Sutton in Ashfield
(Derrick Daines)
18 Cuttings Avenue
Sutton in Ashfield
Notts

Index